Soapmaking
the Natural Way

Soapmaking the Natural Way

45 Melt-and-Pour Recipes
Using Herbs, Flowers & Essential Oils

REBECCA ITTNER

A Division of Sterling Publishing Co., Inc.
New York / London

A Red Lips 4 Courage Communications, Inc. book

www.redlips4courage.com

Eileen Cannon Paulin
President

Catherine Risling
Director of Editorial

Erika Kotite
Development Director

Art Director: Susan H. Hartman

Copy Editor: Catherine Risling

Photographer: Mark Tanner

Photo Stylist: Rebecca Ittner

Library of Congress Cataloging-in-Publication Data

Ittner, Rebecca.
  Soapmaking the natural way : 45 melt-and-pour recipes using herbs, flowers
& essential oils / Rebecca Ittner. -- 1st ed.
      p. cm.
  Includes index.
  ISBN 978-1-60059-601-8 (hc-plc with jacket : alk. paper)
  1. Soap. I. Title.
  TP991.I88 2010
  668'.12--dc22

                                        2009045036

10 9 8 7 6 5 4 3 2 1

First Edition

Published by Lark Crafts, A Division of Sterling Publishing Co., Inc.
387 Park Avenue South, New York, NY 10016
New York / London

Text © 2010, Rebecca Ittner
Photography © 2010, Red Lips 4 Courage Communications, Inc.
Illustrations © 2010, Red Lips 4 Courage Communications, Inc.

Distributed in Canada by Sterling Publishing,
c/o Canadian Manda Group, 165 Dufferin Street
Toronto, Ontario, Canada M6K 3H6

Distributed in the United Kingdom by GMC Distribution Services,
Castle Place, 166 High Street, Lewes, East Sussex, England BN7 1XU

Distributed in Australia by Capricorn Link (Australia) Pty Ltd.,
P.O. Box 704, Windsor, NSW 2756 Australia

If you have questions or comments about this book, please contact:

Lark Crafts
67 Broadway
Asheville, NC 28801
(828) 253-0467

Manufactured in China

ISBN 13: 978-1-60059-601-8

For information about custom editions, special sales, premium and
corporate purchases, please contact Sterling Special Sales Department
at (800) 805-5489 or specialsales@sterlingpub.com.

For information about desk and examination copies available to college and
university professors, requests must be submitted to academic@larkbooks.com.
Our complete policy can be found at www.larkbooks.com.

CONTENTS

INTRODUCTION

Crafters have many interpretations of the term "natural soap crafting." On one end of the spectrum, it can mean using only organic, chemical-free ingredients including soap bases, additives, colorants, and fragrances. On the other end, "natural" can mean simply avoiding animal- or petroleum-based products. For purposes of this book, "natural" means avoiding all animal- and petroleum-based products, synthetic colorants, and fragrances.

To keep the process accessible, I have included melt-and-pour soap bases that contain some additives, because they're widely available in craft stores. The majority of ingredients used in this book—from herbs, dried flowers, and sea salt to milk powders, spices, and essential oils—can be found at craft, grocery, or health food stores. The exceptions to this include clays and colored mica powders. These are inexpensive and can easily be found on the Internet. Mica powders fall in a gray area in the definition of natural. They start out as natural minerals that are mined and ground into powder; synthetic colorants are then added to the powders. I've included mica powders in a few of the projects to show the range of colors they can provide.

Regardless of the interpretation, natural does not mean boring. Beautiful, wonderfully scented soaps can be created with natural ingredients. Mother Nature has gifted us with a wealth of natural colorants and exfoliators. Essential oils, made from plants and botanicals, provide unlimited possibilities for scent combinations.

Melt-and-pour soapmaking is fun and easy. You may even have all the tools you need just sitting in your kitchen. A trip to a local store or two to gather the ingredients and a couple of hours of free time and you're ready to get started.

Handmade soaps make people feel special. Use them throughout your home, wrap them in beautiful boxes, and give them as birthday gifts. You can even create unique soaps for party and wedding favors. Once you try the recipes on the following pages, get creative with the ingredients and make your own soap recipes. Most of all, have fun!

CHAPTER 1

Getting Started

This chapter introduces various types of melt-and-pour soaps and additives, as well as the materials and tools needed to create the soaps featured in this book. You also will learn the simple techniques required to make the projects.

MELT-AND-POUR SOAP

There are many types of melt-and-pour soap bases available today. In keeping with the natural theme of this book, only vegetable-based glycerin soap bases were used in creating the projects in the following chapters. If you want additives to be evenly distributed throughout your finished soap, use a suspension formula soap base. Additives will sink in regular soap bases.

Craft stores are the easiest places to find melt-and-pour soap bases, and they offer a variety of soaps with natural ingredients like olive, avocado, and cucumber oils, as well as shea butter and goat's milk. However, they do include chemical compounds. If you want organic or chemical-free soap bases, an Internet search will yield numerous companies that offer these products.

Craft stores sell soap in 2-pound (908 g) packages that are scored for easy measuring, and in 5- and 20-pound (2.3 and 9 kg) blocks. If you plan on making larger batches of soap, consider purchasing your soap bases from online sellers.

On the next page is a list of common melt-and-pour soap bases and their general benefits.

- **Aloe:** A glycerin-based soap with aloe vera. Soothing to the skin.

- **Avocado cucumber:** A glycerin-based soap with avocado and cucumber extracts. Avocado is moisturizing and rich in vitamin E. Cucumber is an emollient safe for sensitive skin.

- **Clear glycerin:** Made with vegetable oils. To remove any cloudiness from clear glycerin soap, simply melt the soap, let it harden, then re-melt it for use in your soap recipe.

- **Goat's milk:** A glycerin-based soap with goat's milk. Mild and gently moisturizing with a pH level similar to skin's.

- **Olive oil:** A glycerin-based soap with olive oil. Moisturizing to the skin.

- **Shea butter:** A glycerin-based soap with shea butter. Creamy and highly moisturizing to the skin. Lathers well.

- **Soy:** A glycerin-based soap with soy oil. Moisturizing and soothing to the skin.

- **White glycerin:** This clear glycerin soap, with titanium dioxide added to it, gives the soap an opaque white appearance. Titanium dioxide is a natural oxide used as a colorant in soaps, lotions, and foods.

ADDITIVES

Natural additives impart color and texture and infuse melt-and-pour soap with the ability to exfoliate, soothe, and moisturize. These additives include herbs and botanicals, salts, milk powders, oils, nutshells, and kitchen staples such as cornmeal and spices.

Just because an additive is natural does not mean it is safe to use in soapmaking. For instance, you should never use fruit or vegetables in your melt-and-pour soaps because they will spoil quickly, making your soap rancid and unusable.

This section lists natural additives that are safe for soapmaking, and suggests how to use them. If you want to try other natural additives, be sure to research their safety and use before including them in your soaps. Do not use any additives if you are allergic to them.

Like tools, additives should be used for soapmaking only once you've designated them for this use. This protects against cross-contamination.

With few exceptions, the additives used in these projects can be found in craft, grocery, or health food stores.

Exfoliators

There is certainly no shortage of natural exfoliants. Most of them are familiar ingredients in cooking or are used as bath soaks. At left is a list of the most popular.

POPULAR EXFOLIATORS

Blueberry seeds

Coffee grounds

Cornmeal: blue, white, and yellow

Dried chamomile flowers

Dried lavender flowers

Dried lemon peel

Dried lemongrass

Eucalyptus leaves

Green tea leaves

Ground apricot seeds

Ground pumice

Ground walnut shells

Loofah: sliced and shredded

Oatmeal

Peppermint leaves

Poppy seeds

Salts: mineral, sea, Himalayan

Spearmint leaves

Strawberry seeds

Turbanado sugar

Wheat germ

Milk Powders

Milk powder gives soap added benefits. Use 1–2 teaspoons (5–10 ml) per pound (454 ml) of soap. To help incorporate milk powder into melted soap, stir in a bit of water (I prefer using hot water) to the milk powder in a small bowl until you have a thick liquid. Strain the liquid through a strainer or cheesecloth into a second small bowl to remove any lumps.

Sometimes you may still find lumps in your soap after adding a milk paste, especially when using buttermilk. When this happens, strain the melted soap into a glass measuring cup, then continue adding ingredients as needed. Following are the most common milk powders used in melt-and-pour soapmaking and their benefits:

Buttermilk: Increases smoothness of melt-and-pour soaps. Soothing and moisturizing.

Goat's milk: A natural emollient. Soothes and moisturizes. Helps balance the skin's natural pH.

Non-fat milk: A natural emollient. Soothes and moisturizes.

Vegetable Butters and Oils

When added to melt-and-pour soap, oils and butters give soap emollient, humectant, and moisturizing properties. Emollients soften and soothe skin, humectants help skin retain moisture, and moisturizers soften the skin and make it more pliable. Use up to 1 tablespoon (15 ml) of oil or butter per pound (454 ml) of soap. Here are the most common butters and oils used in melt-and-pour soap:

Coconut oil: Increases lather. Virgin coconut oil adds a slight coconut smell to soap.

Jojoba oil: Humectant and moisturizing.

Shea butter: Emollient and moisturizing.

Sweet almond oil: Suitable for all skin types. Emollient. Soothes and softens skin. Increases lather. Helps relieve inflammation, irritation, and itching. Use along with an antioxidant like vitamin E oil.

Vitamin E oil: Natural antioxidant and preservative. Add to soap recipes when using other oils or liquids such as aloe vera.

Colorants

The most natural way to color soaps is with botanicals, herbs, spices, and infused olive oils. The range of colors that can be achieved is limited, though you can still create beautiful soaps using strictly natural colorants. At right is a list of the most popular. The majority of soaps in this book are colored in this way.

COLORANTS

Alfalfa powder—medium green

Annatto seed—yellow-orange (must be steeped in oil first to infuse the oil with color)

Chlorophyll powder—medium greens

Cinnamon—tan to brown (can be an irritant)

Cloves, ground—brown

Cocoa powder—brown

Coffee/coffee grounds—brown to black

Curry powder—yellow

Ginger, ground—light tan

Ground calendula petals—yellow

Ground chamomile—yellow-beige

Kelp powder—green

Paprika—light peach to salmon (can be an irritant)

Poppy seeds—gray to black specks

Pumice, ground—very light gray

Safflower petals—yellow to deep orange

Saffron—yellows

Sage, ground—green

Spirulina powder—blue-green

Titanium dioxide—bright white

Turmeric powder—golden yellow to amber

Wheatgrass powder—green

Floral
jasmine
lavender
neroli
rose
ylang-ylang

Herbal
chamomile
clary sage
eucalyptus
peppermint
rosemary

Spice
black pepper
cinnamon
coriander
ginger
nutmeg
vanilla

Citrus
bergamot
grapefruit
lemon
lime
orange (sweet)
tangerine

Earthy
frankincense
myrrh
patchouli
vetiver

Woodsy
cedarwood
sandalwood

Some essential oils should be avoided during pregnancy. If you have any questions regarding the use of essential oils, contact your health care provider. Oils to avoid during pregnancy include:

- cinnamon
- clary sage
- ginger
- jasmine
- juniper
- lemongrass
- myrrh
- nutmeg
- peppermint
- pine
- rose
- rosemary
- sage

Mica powders start out as naturally occurring minerals that are mined, purified, and crushed into fine powder. The powder then has synthetic colorants added to it, resulting in the colored mica powder. To show a wider range of colors that can be created using mica powder, some of the soaps in this book are colored using mica powders. *Note:* To deepen the color, add more of the ingredient.

Clays

Clays are added to soap for a variety of reasons. Some soften while others have cleansing properties. You may find it easier to incorporate clay into your soap by stirring it with a whisk. Here are the most common clays used in melt-and-pour soapmaking and their benefits:

Kaolin: Pure white kaolin is also called china clay. Known for its absorbing and healing properties. Softens skin. Gives soap a soft, slippery feel so it can be used to create shaving soaps. Orange, pink, and red kaolin clays have been colored with oxides.

Rasshoul: A cleansing clay that draws excess oils from the skin. It's also an astringent. Should only be used in soaps for oily skin.

Sodium bentonite: A highly absorbent clay that pulls oils and toxins from the skin. Gives soap a soft, slippery feel so it can be used to create shaving soaps.

SCENTING YOUR SOAPS

Essential oils are the naturally occurring oils extracted from plants, shrubs, roots, bark, flowers, peelings, and resins, while fragrance oils can be a blend of essential and synthetic oils or purely synthetic. The soaps in this book were scented using natural essential oils.

Essential oils can be broken down two ways: by scent family and by notes. Understanding what scent family a particular essential oil belongs to will help you build a fragrance recipe. For instance, if you want to add a woodsy note to an herbal blend, refer to the list of scent families (at left). Understanding what note category an essential oil belongs to will help you create balanced essential oil blends. Top notes are the main scent of the blend, middle notes enhance top notes, and base notes give depth to the blend. Refer to the list of fragrance notes (see page 15) when building your scents.

Creating essential oil blends to use in your soaps is a personal journey. There are no hard-and-fast rules to blending. You may use one essential oil in a soap recipe, or you may use four or more. It is up to you. Information about essential oil blending abounds in books and on the Internet. Used in quantity, essential oils can irritate skin; try to use no more than 3 teaspoons (15 ml) of essential oil per pound (454 g) of soap.

MATERIALS AND TOOLS

There are no expensive or hard-to-find materials or tools needed for melt-and-pour soapmaking. Do remember that once you use the items to make soap, they should not be used for cooking or baking. Many of the items will retain bits of soap or fragrance that can then be transferred to food. By keeping your soap-making items separate from everyday cooking and serving ware, you will always know what you have; no searching through kitchen cabinets before the creating begins. Hand wash your tools in warm water as soap residue can cause dishwashers to overflow with suds. In addition to a stove and microwave, you will need the following items to make melt-and-pour soap.

- **Double boiler:** Using a double boiler to melt your soap provides longer working times by allowing the soap to stay in a melted stage; this is important when creating soaps with multiple additives. Most of the projects in this book call for a double boiler with a lid.

- **Glass measuring cups:** Heat-resistant glass cups are used to melt soap in a microwave and to pour melted soap into molds.

- **Kitchen scale:** Used to weigh soap before melting.

- **Knives and dough and wavy cutters:** Large knives are used to cut soap and additives, while paring knives can be used to carve soap and clean up edges. Dough cutters are great for slicing loaves of soap and slicing off chunks of soap from bulk packages. Wavy cutters give cut soap an interesting look.

- **Measuring spoons:** Use metal measuring spoons as they are less likely to retain fragrance or color.

- **Mixing spoons:** Used to mix in additives. You can use metal, plastic, or wood, but metal cleans up the easiest.

- **Mortar and pestle:** Used to grind up dried herbs and flowers before adding them to soap.

- **Parchment paper or newspaper:** Used to cover your work space before beginning any project. Protects surfaces and makes clean up a breeze.

- **Rubber spatula:** Used to transfer melted soap from a double boiler into a measuring cup or into soap molds, similar to scraping cake batter from a bowl.

- **Spray bottle filled with rubbing alcohol:** Used to spray the surface of soap to eliminate bubbles and ensure that layers stick together.

Some essential oils may irritate skin. Though the amount of essential oils used in soapmaking is small, if you are sensitive to these oils, you may want avoid them. Oils that may irritate skin include:

- basil
- black pepper
- clove
- cinnamon
- ginger
- lemon
- lemongrass
- peppermint

FRAGRANCE NOTES

Top notes

bergamot	neroli
clary sage	orange
coriander	peppermint
eucalyptus	sage
grapefruit	spearmint
lemon	tea tree
lemongrass	thyme
lime	verbena
mandarin/	
tangerine	

Middle notes

bergamot	lavender
black pepper	lemongrass
chamomile	neroli
coriander	nutmeg
cypress	pine
geranium	rosemary

Base notes

cedarwood	neroli
cinnamon	patchouli
clove	rose
frankincense	sandalwood
ginger	vetiver
jasmine	ylang-ylang
myrrh	

- **Thermometer:** Used to measure the temperature of melted soap or oil when infusing oils with botanical additives. Use a cooking or candy thermometer.

- **Vegetable peeler:** Used to create soap curls and to bevel the edges of soap bars.

- **Vegetable spray:** Used as a mold release.

- **Whisk:** Used to mix in additives.

In addition to soap-making tools, you also will need basic crafting supplies and tools to complete the wrapping projects shown in Chapter 6. These include: adhesives, bags (paper, plastic, or organza), cardstock, craft tape, craft knife and self-healing cutting mat, decorative paper, embellishments, needle and thread, ribbon, rubber stamps and ink, scissors, and tags.

Molds

In addition to actual soap molds, many other household items can serve as molds. Consider having a variety of sizes and styles on hand.

- **Metal baking pans:** Cake, cupcake, brownie, mini bundt cake, and muffin pans are used to create soap loaves and shaped soaps. Choose non-stick pans if possible. Lightly coat the pans with vegetable spray then use a paper towel to remove excess spray. This makes removing soap easier.

- **Plastic candle molds:** Some plastic candle molds can be used for soap, such as floating candle molds. Coat with vegetable spray before using.

- **Plastic candy molds:** Since the plastic used in these molds is not as thick or durable as is used in soap molds, allow your soap to cool and form a thin skin on top, then remove the skin and pour the soap into the mold.

- **Plastic storage containers:** Microwave/dishwasher-safe plastic containers can be used as soap molds. Do not use thin plastic items like to-go containers as hot soap may melt the plastic and cause the soap to spill over.

- **Plastic drawer organizers:** Made of durable plastic and available in a variety of sizes, these containers are perfect for making soap loaves that can be cut into bars.

- **Plastic soap molds:** Made of thick, durable, pliable plastic. Many different sizes and shapes.

- **PVC pipe:** Widely available at hardware stores, PVC pipe is used to make round soap loaves. To use as a soap mold, cover one end with four or more layers of plastic wrap and secure with rubber bands. To ensure a pleasing look to the end of the soap and prevent leaking, make sure the plastic wrap is held tight against the end of the mold. Lightly coat the interior of the PVC pipe with vegetable spray to help the hardened soap release from the mold.

- **Silicone bakeware, ice cube trays, and candle and soap molds:** These are incredibly easy to use. The silicone is pliable and hardened soap does not stick to it, which means soaps pop out easily.

TECHNIQUES

This section covers the basics: melting and pouring soap, layering soap, using additives, infusing oils with colors and scents, and removing soap from molds.

Basic Melt-and-Pour Techniques

Prior to beginning, make sure your work area, and all materials and tools, are clean and dry. Lay out materials and tools, measure additives, and prepare the molds. Once the soap is melted, you will need to work quickly. If you need to use a double boiler for more than one soap in a recipe, be sure to wash and dry it between melting sessions—or consider purchasing two double boilers.

Using a large knife, cut the soap into small cubes. Using the kitchen scale, weigh out the proper amount of soap needed.

1. Place the cubes into the double boiler then cover with a lid. Melt the soap over low to medium heat. Don't allow soap to get hotter than 160° F (71° C); allowing it to get too hot will harden soap and can cause it to smell bad.
2. Once the soap is melted, remove the double boiler from the heat. Stir in additives. Milk powders should be stirred in first, then clays, salts, botanicals, herbs, spices, and micas.
3. Transfer the soap to a glass measuring cup using the rubber spatula. The measuring cup should be large enough so the soap doesn't splash out when stirred.
4. Let the soap cool for a couple of minutes, stirring gently, then add essential oils.
5. Carefully pour the soap into the molds immediately after adding the essential oils.
6. Allow the soap to cool and fully harden. This can take from an hour to several hours, depending on the size of the mold. When the soap is ready, it will easily pop out of the mold. *Note:* When making large loaves of soap, allow the soap to set overnight before removing it from the mold.

MICROWAVE METHOD

1. Place cubes of soap in a large glass measuring cup and melt the soap in 10-second intervals to avoid overheating the soap.
2. Stir in additives as in the stove-top method, ending with the addition of essential oils.
3. Pour the soap into the molds.

Removing Soap from Molds

To remove soap from plastic candle, candy, and soap molds, press the center of the mold with your thumb. The soap should pop out easily. If not, put the mold into the refrigerator for 10 minutes then try again.

To remove soap from plastic drawer organizers and storage containers, pull the sides of the container away from the soap, turn over the container, then gently press the bottom of the container to release the soap.

To remove soap from metal pans, turn the pan over. If the soap doesn't pop out, tap the back of the pan. If the soap still doesn't pop out, put the pan in the freezer for 10 minutes. Fill another pan with hot water, then place the bottom of the pan in the water for a few minutes. The soap should now pop out of the mold.

To remove soap from a PCV pipe mold, cover the bottom end with a kitchen towel. Place one end of a can (such as a vegetable or soup can) on the towel and press down hard. This will push the soap through the other end of the mold.

Soap Success

Allow soap to cool at room temperature—not in a refrigerator or freezer, which would make the soap sweat after it is removed from the mold. Nobody likes sweaty soaps.

After filling the soap molds, pour any leftover soap into spare molds. The soap can be re-melted and used at a later time.

Embedding Objects in Soap

Pour a thin layer of soap in the mold, then spray the surface of the soap with rubbing alcohol to eliminate any bubbles, and add the object. Let layer of soap set. Spray the object with rubbing alcohol, then fill the mold with soap. *Note:* When making soap for children, add only rubber or plastic objects; don't use objects with pointy edges. Never let children 3 years of age or younger use embedded soap.

Embedding Soap in Soap

Leftover soap is great to use in embedded soaps. Pour leftover soap into molds then store the soaps for later use. When you want to make embedded soap, cut the bars of leftover soap into small squares or shapes. You can also embed small shaped soaps into larger bars of soap.

To embed soap, pour a thin layer of soap into a mold, spray the soap's surface with rubbing alcohol to eliminate any bubbles, then place small, shaped, or cut soap pieces into the mold. Spray the soap pieces with rubbing alcohol to prevent air pockets and bubbles. This also helps the layers stick together. Allow a thin skin to form on top of the soap, then pour the remaining melted soap into the mold.

Layering Soap

Pour the first layer of soap into the mold, the spray the soap's surface with rubbing alcohol to eliminate any bubbles. Let a thin skin form on top of the soap. (You should be able to gently run your finger over the surface without getting soap on it.) Spray the surface of the soap with rubbing alcohol (this ensures the layers don't separate later on). Repeat until the mold is filled.

Swirling Soap

Swirling two colors of soap together results in beautiful soaps with unique patterns. To create swirled soap, separately melt two colors of soap and stir in any additives, then pour each color into its own glass measuring cup. Pour the soaps side by side into the mold, pouring each at the same rate. *Note:* In order for this method to be successful, the soaps need to be approximately the same temperature when they're poured into the mold. However, if the soap is too hot, the colors will blend together. To prevent this, allow a thin skin to form on top of each of the soaps, then remove the skin and pour the soaps into the mold.

Using a spoon or single wooden chopstick, gently stir the colors to achieve a swirled effect. Be careful not to stir the soaps too much or you will end up with a single-colored soap. Your swirling skills will improve with practice.

Soap Success

When creating layered or swirled soaps, be sure to use clean spoons when making the different colors of soap. This will prevent unwanted color accidents.

Making Soap Curls

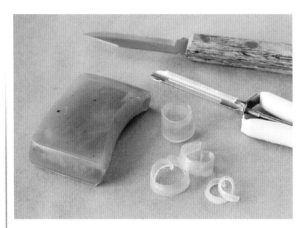

Following desired method, make soap bars. Using a small paring knife or vegetable peeler, cut away thin strips from the edges of the soap. Vary the pressure on the knife or vegetable peeler to create different thicknesses. *Note:* This is also a great way to use up leftover soap.

Embossing Soap with Rubber Stamps

Beginning with a clean mold and rubber stamp, place the rubber stamp faceup on the bottom of the mold. To hold the stamp in place, add a dab of melted soap between the mold and the stamp. Pour the soap into the mold and allow it to cool and fully harden, then remove the soap from the mold. Using the tip of a corsage pin, gently lift one corner of the rubber stamp from the soap, then slowly pull the stamp away from the soap. If necessary, use a paring knife to clean up any edges.

Soap Success

Use only the rubber stamp, not a rubber stamp with a base, when embossing soap. To remove a rubber stamp from a wooden base, carefully cut through the adhesive with a craft knife. Using an adhesive remover, clean the back of the stamp. Wash and dry the stamp before using it with soap.

Infusing Oil

Infusing oil with dried herbs, botanicals, or flowers releases their color and fragrance into the oil. The oil can then be added to melt-and-pour soap. Use 1–2 teaspoons (5–10 ml) of infused oil per pound (454 g) of soap. While annatto seeds were infused in olive oil for use in this book, some other popular choices for this method include dried calendula, chamomile, eucalyptus, lavender, peppermint, rosemary, and sage. Use an oil with very little flavor, such as sunflower, safflower, or extra-virgin olive.

MATERIALS AND TOOLS
Cheesecloth
Cooking or candy thermometer
Double boiler
Dried herbs or flowers: up to ¼ cup (60 ml)
Jar with lid: sterilized
Oil: 1 cup (240 ml)
Strainer

INSTRUCTIONS
1. Combine the herbs and oil in the double boiler and set over low to medium heat.
2. Bring the oil to about 130° F (54.4° C) then let the oil simmer for an hour. *Note:* If you let the oil get too hot, the herbs may cook or the oil may burn.
3. Remove the double boiler from the heat and let it cool a bit. Place three layers of cheesecloth in a strainer and strain the oil into a jar. Make sure to squeeze the last bit of oil into the jar. Seal the jar, let the oil cool, then put it in the refrigerator. If stored in the refrigerator, the oil has a one-month shelf life. *Note:* If you want the oil to have more fragrance or color, repeat this process 1–2 more times.

Soap Success

To prevent introducing bacteria into the infused oil, always use sterilized jars and lids and work on a clean surface. There are a couple of ways to sterilize jars and lids. One way is to run them through a dishwasher cycle, making sure that it is set for high heat wash and dry. Another way is to boil them. To do this, you will need jars and lids, a large pot filled halfway with hot water, tongs, an oven mitt, and paper towels. Using the tongs, carefully place the jars and lids into the hot water. Allow the water to boil for 10 minutes, then turn off the heat. *Note:* Add 1 minute of boiling time for each 1,000 feet (304 m) of elevation.

Wearing the oven mitt and using tongs, remove the jars and lids from the hot water and place them on a double layer of clean paper towels to dry. Store sterilized jars on a clean surface.

CHAPTER 2

Soften and Soothe

Smooth, silky skin is something we all long for. Achieving beautiful skin doesn't have to be expensive or difficult—by using natural, readily available, inexpensive ingredients, you can make soaps that moisturize dry skin, soothe sensitive skin, clean and balance combination skin, and prepare skin for shaving.

The soaps in this chapter have ingredients that do more than clean. With a couple of exceptions, you can find everything you need at grocery or health food stores. The other items can easily be found online. On the following pages you will learn how to make a shaving soap that features kaolin clay; a soothing chamomile bar that has sweet almond and vitamin E oils; and a lavender soap that includes sodium bentonite clay for deep cleaning.

Calming Jasmine and Green Tea

Inspired by a comforting cup of tea, the generous size makes this olive oil soap great for the bath. The amber-colored tea leaves mix beautifully with the earthy green of the wheatgrass powder. Bergamot, jasmine, and sweet orange essential oils give a warm, sensual fragrance to the soap. Sweet almond oil softens the skin. Yields approximately six mini loaves.

MATERIALS

Bergamot essential oil	¼ teaspoon (1.25 ml)
Sweet orange essential oil	½ teaspoon (2.5 ml)
Wheatgrass powder	½ teaspoon (2.5 ml)
Jasmine essential oil	1 teaspoon (5 ml)
Sweet almond oil	1 teaspoon (5 ml)
Dried green tea leaves	½ cup (120 ml)
Olive oil melt-and-pour suspension soap	2 lbs. (908 g)

TOOLS

- Bowl: small
- Double boiler with lid
- Glass measuring cup: 4-cup (960 ml)
- Knife: large
- Measuring spoons
- Metal spoon for stirring
- Mold: mini loaf pan with multiple sections
- Paper towel
- Rubber spatula
- Saucepan: 1 quart (.95 l)
- Spray bottle filled with rubbing alcohol
- Strainer or cheesecloth
- Vegetable spray

INSTRUCTIONS

1. Lightly coat the mini loaf pan with vegetable spray. Using the paper towel, remove any excess spray from the pan.

2. Steep the dried green tea leaves in hot water in the saucepan until the tea is very dark (10 minutes or so). Remove the saucepan from the heat and let cool. Once cool, strain the leaves using the strainer or cheesecloth into the glass bowl. Reserve the leaves and tea for later use.

3. Using the large knife, cut the soap into cubes, then melt the soap in the double boiler, covering the double boiler with the lid.

4. Once the soap is melted, remove the double boiler from the heat. Add 3 tablespoons (45 ml) of the tea leaves to the soap and stir until the tea leaves are evenly distributed throughout the soap. Stir in the sweet almond oil.

5. Add the wheatgrass powder to the melted soap a bit at a time, stirring until the desired color is achieved. Add the essential oils, stirring gently to incorporate.

6. Transfer the soap into the glass measuring cup using the rubber spatula, then pour the soap into the mini loaf pan. Spray the surface of the soap with the rubbing alcohol to eliminate any bubbles.

7. Allow the soap to cool and fully harden, then remove the soap from the pan.

Bamboo Garden

The beauty of this simple soap is its amazing green color, which was created using kelp and turmeric powders. Kelp powder, aloe vera, and vitamin E oil are soothing to the skin. An exotic blend of essential oils is sure to transport you to a peaceful state of mind. Yields approximately four bars.

TOOLS

- Double boiler with lid
- Glass measuring cup: 4-cup (960 ml)
- Knife: large
- Measuring spoons
- Metal spoon for stirring
- Rubber spatula
- Soap molds: round
- Spray bottle filled with rubbing alcohol

MATERIALS

Kelp powder	⅛ teaspoon (.6 ml)
Ginger essential oil	¼ teaspoon (1.25 ml)
Turmeric powder	¼ teaspoon (1.25 ml)
Neroli essential oil	½ teaspoon (2.5 ml)
Sandalwood essential oil	½ teaspoon (2.5 ml)
Aloe vera juice	1 teaspoon (5 ml)
Vitamin E oil	1 teaspoon (5 ml)
Clear glycerin melt-and-pour soap	1 lb. (454 g)

INSTRUCTIONS

1. Using the large knife, cut the soap into cubes, then melt the soap in the double boiler, covering the double boiler with the lid.

2. Once the soap is melted, remove the double boiler from the heat. Add the aloe vera juice and vitamin E oil, stirring gently to incorporate. Stir in the kelp and turmeric powders.

3. Transfer the soap into the glass measuring cup using the rubber spatula, then stir in the essential oils.

4. Pour the soap into the molds, then spray the surface of the soap with rubbing alcohol to eliminate any bubbles.

5. Allow the soap to cool and fully harden, then remove the soap from the molds.

Brown Sugar and Vanilla

This lightly scented soap is wonderfully simple to make. The brown sugar melts to impart a translucent golden brown color and a slightly sweet scent to the glycerin soap—it also increases lather. Vanilla essential oil enhances the sweetness without making the scent overwhelming. Vitamin E oil hydrates the skin—it also has antioxidant properties. Yields up to six bars, depending on thickness.

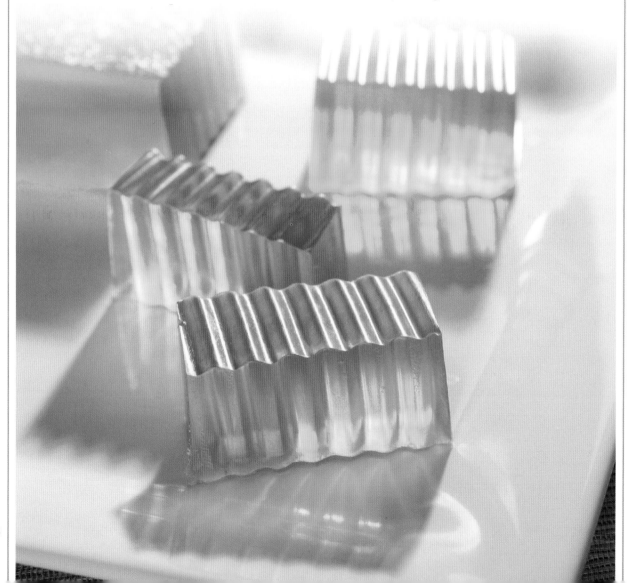

MATERIALS

Vitamin E oil	1 teaspoon (5 ml)
Vanilla essential oil	2 teaspoons (10 ml)
Brown sugar	1½ tablespoons (22 ml)
Clear glycerin melt-and-pour soap	1 lb. (454 g)

TOOLS

- Double boiler with lid
- Dough cutter or wavy cutter
- Glass measuring cup: 4-cup (960 ml)
- Knife: large
- Measuring spoons
- Metal spoon for stirring
- Mold: plastic drawer organizer, 9 × 3 × 2 inches (22 × 7.6 × 5.1 cm)
- Rubber spatula
- Spray bottle filled with rubbing alcohol

INSTRUCTIONS

1 Using the large knife, cut the soap into cubes, then melt the soap in the double boiler, covering the double boiler with the lid.

2 Once the soap is melted, remove the double boiler from the heat, then add the brown sugar and vitamin E oil, stirring gently to incorporate.

3 Transfer the soap into the glass measuring cup using the rubber spatula, then stir in the essential oil. Pour the soap into the mold, then spray the surface of the soap with rubbing alcohol to eliminate any bubbles.

4 Allow the soap to cool and fully harden, then remove the soap from the mold. Using the dough cutter or wavy cutter, cut the soap into bars.

Chamomile Lift

Bergamot and yuzu fruit essential oils give this soap the most
amazing citrus fragrance. Safflower petals and ground chamomile
flowers add a touch of freshness and a rustic look to the soap.
Sweet almond and vitamin E oils moisturize, soothe, and soften
all skin types. The small size of this soap makes it easy to handle
and perfect for a travel bag. Yields approximately four bars.

MATERIALS

Bergamot essential oil	½ teaspoon (2.5 ml)
Safflower petals	½ teaspoon (2.5 ml)
Sweet almond oil	½ teaspoon (2.5 ml)
Vitamin E oil	½ teaspoon (2.5 ml)
Yuzu fruit essential oil	½ teaspoon (2.5 ml)
Chamomile flowers	2 teaspoons (10 ml)
Clear glycerin melt-and-pour soap	1 lb. (454 g)

TOOLS

- Double boiler with lid
- Glass measuring cup: 4-cup (960 ml)
- Knife: large
- Measuring spoons
- Metal spoon for stirring
- Mortar and pestle
- Rubber spatula
- Soap molds: round
- Spray bottle filled with rubbing alcohol

INSTRUCTIONS

1 Using the mortar and pestle, grind up the chamomile flowers. Set aside.

2 Using the large knife, cut the soap into cubes, then melt the soap in the double boiler, covering the double boiler with the lid.

3 Once the soap is melted, remove the double boiler from the heat, then add the ground flowers and safflower petals, stirring gently to incorporate. Stir in the sweet almond and vitamin E oils.

4 Transfer the soap into the glass measuring cup using the rubber spatula, then stir in the essential oils.

5 Pour the soap into the molds, then spray the surface of the soap with rubbing alcohol to eliminate any bubbles.

6 Allow the soap to cool and fully harden, then remove the soap from the molds.

Good Morning
Men's Shave

Turn a morning ritual into a treat for your skin. The bright citrus herbal blend of essential oils is a happy way to greet the day. Bentonite clay helps the razor glide smoothly over the skin, preventing nicks or cuts. You will need a shaving brush to use the soap in the coffee cups. Yields two soap-filled coffee cups.

TOOLS

- Coffee cups: 8 oz. (240 ml) (2)
- Double boiler with lid
- Glass measuring cup: 4-cup (960 ml)
- Knife: large
- Measuring spoons
- Metal spoon or whisk for stirring
- Rubber spatula
- Spray bottle filled with rubbing alcohol

MATERIALS

Rosemary essential oil	¼ teaspoon (1.25 ml)
Jojoba oil	1 teaspoon (5 ml)
Sodium bentonite clay	2 teaspoons (10 ml)
Lime essential oil	2 teaspoons (10 ml)
Avocado cucumber melt-and-pour suspension soap	1 lb. (454 g)

INSTRUCTIONS

1. Wash and dry the coffee cups. Set aside.

2. Using the large knife, cut the soap base into cubes, then melt the soap in the double boiler, covering the double boiler with the lid.

3. Once the soap is melted, remove the double boiler from the heat. Add the sodium bentonite clay and jojoba oil, stirring gently to incorporate.

4. Transfer the soap into the glass measuring cup using the rubber spatula, then stir in the essential oils.

5. Pour the soap into the coffee cups using the rubber spatula, leaving at least 1 inch (2.5 cm) of space between the soap and the top edge of the cups, then spray the surface of the soap with rubbing alcohol to eliminate any bubbles. Allow the soap to cool and fully harden. The shaving soaps are ready to use.

Ladies' Citrus Shave

Shave and treat your skin at the same time. A blend of bergamot, lemon, and lime essential oils lifts the spirits, while jojoba oil gently moisturizes, leaving the skin feeling silky and smooth. Kaolin clay helps the razor glide over the skin for a close, comfortable shave. Yields approximately four bars.

TOOLS

- Double boiler with lid
- Glass measuring cup: 4-cup (960 ml)
- Knife: large
- Measuring spoons
- Metal spoon for stirring
- Mold: square muffin pan
- Rubber spatula
- Spray bottle filled with rubbing alcohol

MATERIALS

Bergamot essential oil	½ teaspoon (2.5 ml)
Lime essential oil	¾ teaspoon (3.75 ml)
Jojoba oil	1 teaspoon (5 ml)
Lemon essential oil	1 teaspoon (5 ml)
Kaolin clay	1 tablespoon (15 ml)
Goat's milk melt-and-pour suspension soap	1 lb. (454 g)

INSTRUCTIONS

1 Using the large knife, cut the soap base into cubes, then melt the soap in the double boiler, covering the double boiler with the lid.

2 Once the soap is melted, remove the double boiler from the heat. Add the kaolin clay and jojoba oil, stirring gently to incorporate.

3 Transfer the soap into the glass measuring cup using the rubber spatula, then stir in the essential oils. Pour the soap into the muffin pan using the rubber spatula.

4 Allow the soap to cool and fully harden, then remove the soap from the pan.

Lavender Clay

Wash your stress away with this lavender-infused soap. While lavender essential oil calms you, sodium bentonite clay absorbs impurities and softens skin, and goat's milk soothes. Crushed lavender flowers color the soap and lend a natural look. Yields approximately four bars.

MATERIALS

Patchouli essential oil	¼ teaspoon (1.25 ml)
Dried lavender flowers	1 teaspoon (5 ml)
Lavender essential oil	1 teaspoon (5 ml)
Vanilla essential oil	1 teaspoon (5 ml)
Sodium bentonite clay	1 tablespoon (15 ml)
Hot water	1 tablespoon (15 ml)
Goat's milk powder	1½ tablespoons (22 ml)
Clear glycerin melt-and-pour soap	1 lb. (454 g)

TOOLS

- Bowls: small (2)
- Double boiler with lid
- Glass measuring cup: 4-cup (960 ml)
- Knife: large
- Measuring spoons
- Metal spoon for stirring
- Mortar and pestle
- Rubber spatula
- Soap molds: rectangle
- Spray bottle filled with rubbing alcohol
- Strainer or cheesecloth

INSTRUCTIONS

1 Using the mortar and pestle, crush the lavender flowers. Set aside.

2 Using the large knife, cut the soap into cubes, then melt the soap in the double boiler, covering the double boiler with the lid.

3 While the soap is melting, mix the goat's milk powder with the hot water in a small bowl. Using a separate bowl and a strainer or cheesecloth, strain the mixture to remove any lumps.

4 Once the soap is melted, remove the double boiler from the heat, then add the goat's milk mixture and sodium bentonite clay, stirring gently to incorporate. Stir in the crushed lavender flowers.

5 Transfer the soap into the glass measuring cup using the rubber spatula, then stir in the essential oils.

6 Pour the soap into the molds, then spray the surface of the soap with rubbing alcohol to eliminate any bubbles.

7 Allow the soap to cool and fully harden, then remove the soap from the molds.

Mint Chocolate

Pure peppermint and eucalyptus essential oils give this pretty soap a refreshing aroma. Eucalyptus oil is known for its antiseptic and anti-inflammatory properties, peppermint for its minty scent and cooling feel. Cocoa powder gives the soap its chocolaty color. Use this soap to unwind in the bath after a long day. Yields approximately four bars.

MATERIALS

Blue mica powder	¼ teaspoon (1.25 ml)
Eucalyptus essential oil	¼ teaspoon (1.25 ml)
Green mica powder	¼ teaspoon (1.25 ml)
Cocoa powder	1 teaspoon (5 ml)
Coconut oil	1 teaspoon (5 ml)
Peppermint essential oil	1 teaspoon (5 ml)
Vanilla essential oil	1 teaspoon (5 ml)
Crushed peppermint leaves	2 teaspoons (10 ml)
Peppermint leaves	1 tablespoon (15 ml)
Avocado cucumber melt-and-pour suspension soap	½ lb. (227 g)
Clear glycerin melt-and-pour soap	½ lb. (227 g)

TOOLS

- Double boiler with lid
- Glass measuring cups: 4-cup (960 ml) (2)
- Knife: large
- Measuring spoons
- Metal spoons for stirring (2)
- Mold: mini loaf pan with multiple sections
- Paper towel
- Plastic wrap
- Rubber spatula
- Spray bottle filled with rubbing alcohol
- Vegetable spray

INSTRUCTIONS

1 Spray the mini loaf pan with vegetable spray, then wipe off the excess spray using the paper towel. Set aside.

2 Using the large knife, cut the clear glycerin soap into cubes, then melt the soap in the double boiler, covering the double boiler with the lid. Once the soap is melted, remove the double boiler from the heat, then add the coconut oil and cocoa powder, stirring gently to incorporate. Transfer the soap into a glass measuring cup using the rubber spatula, then stir in the essential oils. Cover the measuring cup with plastic wrap. *Note:* Covering the cup with plastic wrap helps prevent a skin from forming on top of the soap.

3 Using the large knife, cut the avocado-cucumber soap into cubes, then place the cubes in the glass measuring cup. Cover the glass measuring cup with plastic wrap, then melt the soap in a microwave.

4 Once the soap is melted, add the mica powders, stirring gently to incorporate. Stir in the peppermint leaves, then cover the measuring cup with plastic wrap.

5 Pour the glycerin soap into the molds until the molds are about half full, then spray the surface of the soap with rubbing alcohol to eliminate any bubbles. *Note:* You may have to reheat the soap before pouring it into the molds.

6 Wait until a thin skin forms on top of the glycerin soap, then pour the avocado cucumber soap over the glycerin soap. Sprinkle the crushed peppermint leaves on top of the soap.

7 Allow the soap to cool and fully harden, then remove the soap from the pan.

Vanilla Sundae

Cocoa is swirled with vanilla to create this sweet-smelling, guilt-free treat. Goat's milk softens and soothes the skin, sweet almond oil lightly moisturizes, and the humectant properties of the honey hold in the moisture, making this a great soap for dry, sensitive skin. Yields approximately four bars.

MATERIALS

Cocoa powder	1 teaspoon (5 ml)
Sweet almond oil	1 teaspoon (5 ml)
Vanilla essential oil	1 teaspoon (5 ml)
Honey	2 teaspoons (10 ml)
Goat's milk powder	1 tablespoon (15 ml)
Hot water	1 tablespoon (15 ml)
Clear glycerin melt-and-pour soap	½ lb. (227 g)
Shea butter melt-and-pour suspension soap	½ lb. (227 g)

TOOLS

- Bowls: small (2)
- Double boiler with lid
- Glass measuring cup: 4-cup (960 ml)
- Knife: large
- Measuring spoons
- Metal spoon or whisk for stirring
- Plastic wrap
- Rubber spatula
- Soap molds: rectangle
- Spray bottle filled with rubbing alcohol
- Strainer or cheesecloth
- Toothpicks

INSTRUCTIONS

1 Using the large knife, cut the shea butter soap into cubes, then melt the soap in the double boiler, covering the double boiler with the lid.

2 While the soap is melting, mix the goat's milk powder with the hot water in a small bowl. Using a separate bowl and a strainer or cheesecloth, strain the mixture to remove any lumps.

3 Once the soap is melted, remove the double boiler from the heat. Add the goat's milk mixture and sweet almond oil, stirring gently to incorporate. Transfer the soap into a glass measuring cup using the rubber spatula, then stir in the essential oils. Cover the measuring cup with plastic wrap.

4 Using the large knife, cut the clear glycerin soap into cubes, then melt the soap in the double boiler, covering it with the lid.

5 Once the soap is melted, remove the double boiler from the heat. Add the honey, stirring gently to incorporate. Stir in the cocoa powder. *Note:* You may find that it is easier to incorporate the cocoa powder if you stir it with a whisk.

6 Pour the shea butter soap into the molds until the molds are about half full, then spray the surface of the soap with rubbing alcohol to eliminate any bubbles. *Note:* You will have to reheat the soap in the microwave oven before pouring it into the molds.

7 Pour the glycerin soap in a wavy pattern on top of the shea butter soap. Using the toothpicks, swirl the colors together. Spray the surface of the soap with rubbing alcohol to eliminate any bubbles.

8 Allow the soap to cool and fully harden, then remove the soap from the molds.

Tangerine Dream

This easy layered soap is colored using turmeric powder. Tangerine and sweet orange essential oils make taking a bath with these pretty bars an enjoyable experience. Sweet almond oil lightly moisturizes, leaving your skin feeling soft to the touch. Yields approximately four bars.

MATERIALS

Sweet orange essential oil	½ teaspoon (2.5 ml)
Sweet almond oil	1 teaspoon (5 ml)
Tangerine essential oil	1 teaspoon (5 ml)
Turmeric powder	1¼ teaspoon (6.25 ml)
Goat's milk melt-and-pour suspension soap	1 lb. (454 g)

TOOLS

- Double boiler with lid
- Glass measuring cups: 4-cup (960 ml) (2)
- Knife: large
- Measuring spoons
- Metal spoons for stirring
- Plastic wrap
- Soap molds: rectangle with rounded top
- Spray bottle filled with rubbing alcohol

INSTRUCTIONS

1. Using the large knife, cut the soap into cubes, then melt the soap in the double boiler, covering the double boiler with the lid.

2. Once the soap is melted, remove the double boiler from the heat. Stir in the sweet almond and essential oils, then pour half of the melted soap into each of the measuring cups. Cover one measuring cup with plastic wrap and set aside.

3. Add 1 teaspoon (5 ml) turmeric powder to the uncovered measuring cup, stirring gently to incorporate. Pour an even amount of soap into each mold, then spray the surface of the soap with rubbing alcohol to eliminate any bubbles.

4. Add ¼ teaspoon (1.25 ml) turmeric powder to the remaining measuring cup, stirring gently to incorporate. Allow a thin skin to form on top of the soap in the molds, spray the surface of the soap with rubbing alcohol (this ensures that the layers will stick together), then pour the soap into the molds. Spray the surface of the soap with rubbing alcohol.

5. Allow the soap to cool and fully harden, then remove the soap from the molds.

Cedar Forest

Bring back memories of your last walk in the woods with this cedarwood-scented soap. Kaolin clay and jojoba oil soften the skin. Tea tree essential oil is known to soothe irritated skin, including bug bites and scrapes. Because the tea tree and cedarwood aromas are strong, only the green-colored embeds are scented. Yields six to eight bars, depending on size.

MATERIALS

Wheatgrass	⅛ teaspoon (.6 ml)
Tea tree essential oil	½ teaspoon (2.5 ml)
Jojoba oil	1 teaspoon (5 ml)
Cedarwood essential oil	2 teaspoons (10 ml)
Kaolin clay	1 tablespoon (15 ml)
Chlorophyll powder	1 gel capsule
Kelp powder	1 gel capsule
Clear glycerin melt-and-pour soap	1½ lbs. (682 g)

TOOLS

- Double boiler with lid
- Glass measuring cups: 4-cup (960 ml) (3)
- Knife: large
- Measuring spoons
- Metal spoons for stirring (2)
- Mold: plastic drawer organizers, 9 × 3 × 2 inches (22 × 7.6 × 5.1 cm) (2)
- Plastic wrap
- Rubber spatula
- Spray bottle filled with rubbing alcohol
- Wavy cutter

INSTRUCTIONS

1 Using the large knife, cut the soap into cubes, then melt the soap in the double boiler, covering the double boiler with the lid.

2 Once the soap is melted, remove the double boiler from the heat, then stir in the kaolin clay and jojoba oil. Pour equal amounts of the melted soap into each of the measuring cups using the rubber spatula. Cover one of the measuring cups with plastic wrap and set aside.

3 Open the chlorophyll and kelp powder gel capsules. To one of the remaining measuring cups, stir in ⅛ teaspoon (.6 ml) chlorophyll powder, ¼ teaspoon (1.25 ml) kelp powder, and the wheatgrass, then stir in the essential oils. Into the other remaining measuring cup, stir in 1 teaspoon (.6 ml) chlorophyll powder.

4 Pour one colored soap into each mold, then spray the surface of the soaps with rubbing alcohol to eliminate any bubbles. Allow the soaps to cool and fully harden, then remove the soaps from the mold. Cut the colored soaps into varying sizes.

5 Reheat the uncolored soap, then pour a small amount of it into the mold. Allow the soap to cool until a thin skin forms on top of the soap. Remove the skin, arrange the cut pieces on top of the soap, then spray them generously with rubbing alcohol. Pour the remainder of the uncolored soap into the mold, then spray the top of the soap with rubbing alcohol.

6 Allow the soap to cool and fully harden, then remove the soap from the mold. Cut the soap into bars using the wavy cutter.

CHAPTER 3

Exfoliate

From seeds and ground nut shells to cornmeal and sea salt, natural exfoliants work wonders. When choosing nature's scrubbers to use in your soaps, consider what purpose the soap will serve. For foot scrubs, blueberry seeds, Dead Sea salt, and ground pumice are hard-working choices. To clean hands after a day in the garden, ground pumice, cornmeal, and fine-grain mineral or sea salt deep clean but won't scratch the skin. For the face, use extra gentle exfoliants like oatmeal and wheat germ.

In this chapter you will learn how to make soaps that take cleaning to a deeper level using a variety of natural polishers. To prevent dryness, the recipes also contain ingredients to leave skin lightly moisturized. Scrub away kitchen dirt and smells with coffee grounds, slough off dry skin and refresh your feet with Dead Sea salt, and enjoy a great smelling poppy seed soap that offers a gentle scrub.

Milk and Honey

Soothing and gently exfoliating, this creamy bar has the comforting scent of vanilla. Buttermilk and oatmeal have long been touted as being great for soothing and moisturizing sensitive skin. If you prefer a smooth appearance to your soaps, stir in all of the oatmeal before pouring the soap into the pan. Yields approximately eight bars.

MATERIALS

Vanilla essential oil	■	2 teaspoons (10 ml)
Honey	■	1 tablespoon (15 ml)
Buttermilk powder	■	2 tablespoons (30 ml)
Hot water	■	2 tablespoons (30 ml)
Oatmeal (do not use quick-cooking oatmeal)	■	1 cup (240 ml)
Shea butter melt-and-pour suspension soap	■	2 lbs. (908 g)

TOOLS

- Bowls: small (2)
- Double boiler with lid
- Glass measuring cup: 4-cup (960 ml)
- Knife: large
- Measuring spoons
- Metal spoon for stirring
- Mold: square muffin or brownie pan with multiple sections
- Paper towel
- Rubber spatula
- Spray bottle filled with rubbing alcohol
- Strainer or cheesecloth
- Vegetable spray

INSTRUCTIONS

1 Lightly coat the pan with vegetable spray. Using a paper towel, remove any excess spray.

2 Using the large knife, chop the oatmeal so the flakes are about half their original size.

3 Sprinkle about 1 teaspoon (5 ml) of the chopped oatmeal evenly on the bottom of each square in the pan.

4 Using the large knife, cut the soap into cubes, then melt the soap in the double boiler, covering the double boiler with the lid.

5 While the soap is melting, mix the buttermilk powder with the hot water in a small bowl. Using a separate bowl and a strainer or cheesecloth, strain the mixture to remove any lumps.

6 Once the soap is melted, add the buttermilk mixture and honey, stirring gently to incorporate. Stir in ¾ cup (180 ml) of oatmeal until it is evenly distributed, then stir in the essential oil.

7 Transfer the soap into the glass measuring cup using the rubber spatula. Slowly pour the soap into the pan, then spray the surface of the soap with rubbing alcohol to eliminate any bubbles.

8 Allow the soap to cool and fully harden, then remove the soap from the pan.

Berry Smoothie

Blueberries are good for you inside and out. This soap contains blueberry seeds that make it a surprisingly heavy-duty scrub, so avoid using it on the face or on sensitive skin. Yields approximately six oversized bars.

MATERIALS

Black mica powder	1 pinch
Vanilla essential oil	¼ teaspoon (1.25 ml)
Blue mica powder	1 teaspoon (5 ml)
Purple mica powder	1½ teaspoons (7.5 ml)
Black raspberry essential oil, divided in half	2½ teaspoons (12.5 ml)
Blueberry seeds	3 tablespoons (45 ml)
Shea butter melt-and-pour suspension soap, divided in half	2 lbs. (908 g)

TOOLS

- Double boiler with lid
- Dough cutter
- Glass measuring cups: 4-cup (960 ml) (2)
- Knife: large
- Measuring spoons
- Metal spoon for stirring
- Mold: plastic drawer organizer, 9 × 6 × 2 inches (22 × 15.2 × 5.1 cm)
- Plastic wrap
- Rubber spatula
- Spray bottle filled with rubbing alcohol

INSTRUCTIONS

1 Using the large knife, cut the soap into cubes. Melt 1 lb. (454 g) of soap in the double boiler, covering the double boiler with the lid.

2 Once the soap is melted, remove the double boiler from the heat, then add the mica powders, stirring gently to incorporate. Stir in the blueberry seeds.

3 Transfer the soap into a glass measuring cup using the rubber spatula, then stir in the vanilla essential oil and 1¼ teaspoons (6.25 ml) black raspberry essential oil. Cover the measuring cup with plastic wrap.

4 In a microwave oven, melt 1 lb. (454 g) of soap in the remaining measuring cup, covering the cup with plastic wrap prior to melting the soap.

5 Once the soap is melted, add 1¼ teaspoons (6.25 ml) black raspberry essential oil, stirring gently to incorporate.

6 Pour the soaps side by side into the mold, then spray the surface of the soap with rubbing alcohol to eliminate any bubbles. Swirl the two colors together (see page 19), then spray the surface of the soap with rubbing alcohol.

7 Allow the soap to cool and fully harden. Remove the soap from the mold, then cut into bars using the dough cutter.

Cornmeal and Wheat Germ Scrub

This soap is great for anyone with rough, dry hands. Cornmeal and wheat germ gently exfoliate the skin, while honey and goat's milk moisturize and soften. Layering imparts an interesting look to the warm herbal-scented soap. Yields approximately four to six bars.

MATERIALS

Bergamot essential oil	▪	⅛ teaspoon (.6 ml)
Lavender essential oil	▪	½ teaspoon (2.5 ml)
Honey	▪	1 teaspoon (5 ml)
Sandalwood essential oil	▪	1 teaspoon (5 ml)
Goat's milk powder	▪	1 tablespoon (15 ml)
Hot water	▪	1 tablespoon (15 ml)
Wheat germ	▪	1 tablespoon (15 ml)
Hot water	▪	1½ tablespoons (22 ml)
Yellow cornmeal, divided in half	▪	2 tablespoons (30 ml)
Olive oil melt-and-pour suspension soap	▪	½ lb. (227 g)
Shea butter melt-and-pour suspension soap	▪	½ lb. (227 g)

TOOLS

- Bowls: small (2)
- Double boiler with lid
- Glass measuring cups: 4-cup (960 ml) (2)
- Knife: large
- Measuring spoons
- Metal spoon or whisk for stirring
- Plastic wrap
- Rubber spatula
- Soap molds: rectangle and octagon
- Spray bottle filled with rubbing alcohol
- Strainer or cheesecloth

INSTRUCTIONS

1   Using the large knife, cut the shea butter soap into cubes, then melt it in the double boiler, covering the double boiler with the lid.

2   While the soap base is melting, mix the goat's milk powder with the hot water in a small bowl. Using a separate bowl and a strainer or cheesecloth, strain the mixture to remove any lumps.

3   Once the soap is melted, remove the double boiler from the heat. Add the goat's milk mixture, 1 tablespoon (15 ml) yellow cornmeal, and 1 tablespoon (15 ml) wheat germ, stirring gently to incorporate. Transfer the soap into a glass measuring cup using the rubber spatula, then stir in the essential oils. Cover the measuring cup with plastic wrap.

4   Using the large knife, cut the olive oil soap into cubes, then place the cubes in the glass measuring cup. Cover the glass measuring cup with plastic wrap, then melt the soap in a microwave.

5   Once the soap is melted, add the honey, stirring gently to incorporate. Stir in 1 tablespoon (15 ml) yellow cornmeal.

6   Beginning with the olive oil soap, layer the two soap mixtures into the molds (see page 19). Spray the surface of the soap with rubbing alcohol between layers to remove any bubbles and to ensure the layers will stick together. When the molds are filled, spray the surface of the soap with rubbing alcohol to eliminate any bubbles.

7   Allow the soap to cool and fully harden, then remove the soap from the molds.

Lemon Poppy Seed Muffin

These muffin-shaped soaps smell just like the real thing. Dried lemon peel and poppy seeds soften and refresh rough, dry skin. When mixed with white shea butter soap, turmeric powder gives a light lemon-yellow color. Yields approximately three bars.

TOOLS

- Double boiler with lid
- Glass measuring cup: 4-cup (960 ml)
- Knife: large
- Measuring spoons
- Metal spoon for stirring
- Mold: silicone muffin pan
- Rubber spatula
- Spray bottle filled with rubbing alcohol

MATERIALS

Vanilla essential oil	¼ teaspoon (1.25 ml)
Dried lemon peel	1 teaspoon (5 ml)
Lemon essential oil	1 teaspoon (5 ml)
Turmeric powder	1 teaspoon (5 ml)
Poppy seeds	2 teaspoons (10 ml)
Shea butter melt-and-pour suspension soap	½ lb. (227 g)

INSTRUCTIONS

1 Using the large knife, cut the soap into cubes, then melt the soap in the double boiler, covering the double boiler with the lid.

2 Once the soap is melted, remove the double boiler from the heat. Add the turmeric powder, stirring gently to incorporate. Stir in the dried lemon peel and poppy seeds.

3 Transfer the soap into the glass measuring cup using the rubber spatula, then stir in the essential oils.

4 Pour the soap into the muffin pan, then spray the surface of the soap with rubbing alcohol to eliminate any bubbles.

5 Allow the soap to cool and fully harden, then remove the soap from the muffin pan.

Ocean Breeze

Dead Sea salt infuses this soap with a high concentration of minerals that helps keep skin soft and hydrated. The minerals are also believed to encourage healing. A blend of mica powders and kelp color the soap a beautiful Caribbean blue. The clean, invigorating ocean scent gives a unisex appeal. Yields approximately four bars.

TOOLS

- Double boiler with lid
- Glass measuring cup: 4-cup (960 ml)
- Knife: large
- Measuring spoons
- Metal spoon for stirring
- Rubber spatula
- Soap molds: various shapes
- Spray bottle filled with rubbing alcohol

MATERIALS

Green mica powder	⅛ teaspoon (.6 ml)
Lemongrass essential oil	⅛ teaspoon (.6 ml)
Blue mica powder	¼ teaspoon (1.25 ml)
Vitamin E oil	¼ teaspoon (1.25 ml)
Jojoba oil	½ teaspoon (2.5 ml)
Tea tree essential oil	½ teaspoon (2.5 ml)
Cedarwood essential oil	1 teaspoon (5 ml)
Dead Sea salt	2 tablespoons (30 ml) plus ¼ cup (60 ml)
Kelp powder	2 gel capsules
Olive oil melt-and-pour suspension soap	1 lb. (454 g)

INSTRUCTIONS

1 Using the large knife, cut the soap into cubes, then melt the soap in the double boiler, covering the double boiler with the lid.

2 Once the soap is melted, remove the double boiler from the heat. Add the jojoba and vitamin E oils, stirring gently to incorporate. Open the gel capsules, then add the kelp powder to the soap, stirring gently to incorporate. Stir in the mica powders, then add ¼ cup (60 ml) Dead Sea salt.

3 Transfer the soap into the glass measuring cup using the rubber spatula, then stir in the essential oils.

4 Pour a thin layer of the soap into the molds, then sprinkle a layer of Dead Sea salt onto the layer of soap. Spray the surface of the soap with rubbing alcohol to eliminate any bubbles.

5 Gently stir the remaining soap in the measuring cup and finish filling the molds. *Note:* Even with suspension soaps, the heavy salts will sink, so you will have to help the Dead Sea salt into the molds using the spoon or rubber spatula. Spray the surface of the soap with rubbing alcohol to eliminate any bubbles.

6 Allow the soap to cool and fully harden, then remove the soap from the molds.

Spicy Floral Scrub

This moisturizing soap gives just a light scrub. Strawberry seeds and ground cloves create the speckled appearance. If you prefer a more vigorous exfoliator, simply add more strawberry seeds. A slightly spicy blend of essential oils makes this a great soap for both men and women. Yields approximately two bars.

MATERIALS

Ground cloves	½ teaspoon (2.5 ml)
Clove essential oil	1 teaspoon (5 ml)
Ylang-ylang essential oil	1 teaspoon (5 ml)
Coral mica powder	1 teaspoon (5 ml)
Strawberry seeds	2 teaspoons (10 ml)
Shea butter melt-and-pour suspension soap	½ lb. (228 g)

TOOLS

Double boiler with lid

Glass measuring cup: 4-cup (960 ml)

Knife: large

Measuring spoons

Metal spoon for stirring

Rubber spatula

Soap molds: rectangle

Spray bottle filled with rubbing alcohol

INSTRUCTIONS

1 Using the large knife, cut the soap into cubes, then melt the soap in the double boiler, covering the double boiler with the lid.

2 Once the soap is melted, remove the double boiler from the heat. Add the mica powder, ground cloves, and strawberry seeds, stirring gently to incorporate.

3 Transfer the soap into the glass measuring cup using the rubber spatula, then stir in the essential oils.

4 Pour the soap into the molds, then spray the surface of the soap with rubbing alcohol to eliminate any bubbles.

5 Allow the soap to cool and fully harden, then remove the soap from the molds.

Caffè Latte

Cooks and coffee lovers are sure to love this hard-working soap that exfoliates dry skin as it soothes and moisturizes. And it smells good enough to drink. Vanilla-flavored coffee grounds scrub hands clean and absorb kitchen smells like fish and garlic. The addition of goat's milk powder ensures soft hands. Yields up to 12 bars, depending on thickness.

MATERIALS

Honey	■	2 teaspoons (10 ml)
Coffee (see instructions)	■	1 tablespoon (15 ml)
Vanilla essential oil, divided in half	■	1 tablespoon (15 ml)
Vanilla-flavored coffee grounds	■	2 tablespoons (30 ml)
Goat's milk powder	■	2 tablespoons (30 ml)
Hot water	■	2 tablespoons (30 ml)
Goat's milk melt-and-pour suspension soap	■	2 lbs. (908 g)

TOOLS

- Bowls: small (2)
- Double boiler with lid
- Dough cutter or wavy cutter
- Glass measuring cups: 4-cup (960 ml) (2)
- Knife: large
- Measuring spoons
- Metal spoons for stirring (2)
- Mold: small loaf pan
- Rubber spatula
- Spray bottle filled with rubbing alcohol
- Strainer or cheesecloth

INSTRUCTIONS

1 Make one cup of hot coffee using the flavored coffee grounds. Set aside.

2 Using the large knife, cut the soap into cubes, then melt the soap in the double boiler, covering the double boiler with the lid.

3 While the soap is melting, mix the goat's milk powder with the hot water in a small bowl. Using a separate bowl and a strainer or cheesecloth, strain the mixture to remove any lumps.

4 Once the soap is melted, remove the double boiler from the heat. Pour an even amount of soap into each measuring cup using the rubber spatula.

5 Add the goat's milk mixture and honey in one of the measuring cups, stirring gently to incorporate. Stir in 1½ teaspoons (7.5 ml) vanilla essential oil.

6 Add the coffee and coffee grounds in the other measuring cup, stirring gently to incorporate. Stir in 1½ teaspoons (7.5 ml) vanilla essential oil.

7 Pour the soaps side by side into the loaf pan, then spray the surface of the soap with rubbing alcohol to eliminate any bubbles. Swirl the two colors together (see page 19), then spray the surface of the soap with rubbing alcohol.

8 Allow the soap to cool and fully harden. Remove the soap from the pan, then cut into bars using the dough cutter or wavy cutter.

Himalayan Magic

Himalayan pink salt, mined near the base of the Himalayan Mountains, softens and soothes the skin. Its natural color creates a light pink soap without the addition of any other colorants. Gentle enough to be used on the entire body, this soap smells like a rose in full bloom. Yields approximately four to six bars.

TOOLS

- Double boiler with lid
- Glass measuring cup: 4-cup (960 ml)
- Knife: large
- Measuring spoons
- Metal spoon for stirring
- Rubber spatula
- Soap molds: rectangle, square
- Spray bottle filled with rubbing alcohol

MATERIALS

Patchouli essential oil	¼ teaspoon (1.25 ml)
Geranium essential oil	½ teaspoon (2.5 ml)
Rose essential oil	1 teaspoon (5 ml)
Himalayan pink salt	2 tablespoons (30 ml)
Olive oil melt-and-pour suspension soap	1 lb. (454 g)

INSTRUCTIONS

1 Using the large knife, cut the soap into cubes, then melt the soap in the double boiler, covering the double boiler with the lid.

2 Once the soap is melted, remove the double boiler from the heat. Add the Himalayan pink salt, stirring gently to incorporate. Transfer the soap into the glass measuring cup using the rubber spatula, then stir in the essential oils.

3 Pour the soap into the molds using the rubber spatula, then spray the surface of the soap with rubbing alcohol to eliminate any bubbles.

4 Allow the soap to cool and fully harden, then remove the soap from the molds.

Pretty Feet Bar

Your feet work hard so take the time to give them some special attention. This soap contains ground pumice and mineral salt to scrub away dirt and grime, leaving your tootsies feeling smooth and relaxed. Use this soap after a long day on your feet or before a pedicure. Yields up to six bars, depending on thickness.

MATERIALS

Peppermint essential oil	⅛ teaspoon (.6 ml)
Eucalyptus essential oil	½ teaspoon (2.5 ml)
Tea tree essential oil	½ teaspoon (2.5 ml)
Dried peppermint leaves, crushed	1 teaspoon (5 ml)
Wheatgrass powder	1 teaspoon (5 ml)
Fine-grain mineral salt	1 tablespoon (15 ml)
Ground pumice	2 tablespoons (30 ml)
Kelp powder	2 gel capsules
Shea butter melt-and-pour suspension soap	1 lb. (454 g)

TOOLS

- Double boiler with lid
- Dough cutter or wavy cutter
- Glass measuring cup: 4-cup (960 ml)
- Knife: large
- Measuring spoons
- Metal spoon for stirring
- Mold: plastic drawer organizer, 9 × 3 × 2 inches (22 × 7.6 × 5.1 cm)
- Rubber spatula
- Small metal spoon or whisk for stirring
- Spray bottle filled with rubbing alcohol

INSTRUCTIONS

1 Using the large knife, cut the soap into cubes, then melt the soap in the double boiler, covering the double boiler with the lid.

2 Once the soap is melted, remove the double boiler from the heat. Open the kelp powder gel capsules, then add the kelp powder, stirring gently to incorporate. Stir in the ground pumice, wheatgrass powder, dried peppermint leaves, and mineral salt.

3 Transfer the soap into the glass measuring cup using the rubber spatula, then stir in the essential oils.

4 Pour the soap into the mold using the rubber spatula. Spray the surface of the soap with rubbing alcohol to eliminate any bubbles.

5 Allow the soap to cool and fully harden, then remove the soap from the mold. Using the dough cutter or wavy cutter, cut the soap into bars.

Pomegranate Crush

This yummy-smelling soap gently exfoliates using shredded loofah. Because the loofah will float to the surface, you need to pour the soap in layers so the shreds are distributed evenly throughout each bar. Red mica powder creates a beautiful pomegranate color when added to the olive oil soap. Yields two bars.

Red mica powder	▪	½ teaspoon (2.5 ml)
Pomegranate essential oil	▪	1 teaspoon (5 ml)
Vanilla essential oil	▪	1 teaspoon (5 ml)
Shredded loofah	▪	2 tablespoons (30 ml)
Olive oil melt-and-pour suspension soap	▪	½ lb. (227 g)

TOOLS

- Glass measuring cup: 4-cup (960 ml)
- Knife: large
- Measuring spoons
- Metal spoon for stirring
- Plastic wrap
- Scissors: large
- Soap molds: oval
- Spray bottle filled with rubbing alcohol

INSTRUCTIONS

1   Using the large knife, cut a chunk off the loofah, the same way corn is cut from the cob. From the top, run the knife along the spine of the loofah. Using the scissors, cut the chunk in small pieces.

2   Using the large knife, cut the soap into cubes, then place the cubes in the glass measuring cup. Cover the cup with plastic wrap, then melt the soap in a microwave.

3   Once the soap is melted, add the mica powder, stirring gently to incorporate. Stir in the essential oils, then add the shredded loofah, stirring to blend.

4   Pour the soap mixture into the molds, filling the molds about one-third full. Spray the surface of the soap with rubbing alcohol to eliminate any bubbles. Let a thin skin form on the soap, spray the surface of the soap with rubbing alcohol again (this ensures that the layers will not separate), then fill the molds two-thirds full. Repeat once more until the mold is filled, then spray the surface of the soap with rubbing alcohol. *Note:* Stir the soap in the glass measuring cup between pouring the layers to ensure that there will be loofah in each layer.

5   Allow the soap to cool and fully harden, then remove the soap from the molds.

Gardener's Clean-Up

Gardening may be good for the soul, but it can be tough on the hands. This embossed soap contains apricot seeds, kaolin clay, and pumice to gently scrub away the dirt, and goat's milk powder and sweet almond oil to moisturize the skin. If you want a deeper green hue, add more chlorophyll powder to the melted soap. Yields approximately three bars.

MATERIALS

Orange essential oil	½ teaspoon (2.5 ml)
Rosemary essential oil	½ teaspoon (2.5 ml)
Lavender essential oil	1 teaspoon (5 ml)
Sweet almond oil	1 teaspoon (5 ml)
Kaolin clay	2 teaspoons (10 ml)
Ground apricot seeds	1 tablespoon (15 ml)
Ground pumice	1 tablespoon (15 ml)
Goat's milk powder	2 tablespoons (30 ml)
Hot water	2 tablespoons (30 ml)
Chlorophyll powder	1 gel capsule
White glycerin melt-and-pour soap	1 lb. (454 g)

TOOLS

- Corsage pin
- Double boiler with lid
- Glass bowls: small (2)
- Glass measuring cup: 4-cup (960 ml)
- Knives: large and paring
- Measuring spoons
- Plastic soap molds: square
- Rubber spatula
- Rubber stamps
- Spray bottle filled with rubbing alcohol
- Strainer or cheesecloth

INSTRUCTIONS

1 Mix the goat's milk and the hot water in a small bowl. Using a separate bowl and a strainer or cheesecloth, strain the mixture to remove any lumps.

2 Using the large knife, cut the soap into cubes, then melt the soap in the double boiler, covering the double boiler with the lid. As the soap is melting, prepare the soap molds with the rubber stamps (see page 20).

3 Once the soap is melted, remove the double boiler from the heat, then add the goat's milk powder and sweet almond oil, stirring gently to incorporate. Open the chlorophyll powder gel capsule, then mix in the powder a bit at a time until the desired color is reached. Add the kaolin clay and ground pumice to the soap, stirring gently to incorporate. Stir in the ground apricot seeds.

4 Transfer the soap into the glass measuring cup using the rubber spatula, then stir in the essential oils. Pour the soap into the molds, then spray the surface of the soap with rubbing alcohol to eliminate any bubbles.

5 Allow the soap to cool and fully harden, then remove the soap from the molds. Working on one soap at a time, gently lift one corner of the rubber stamp with the tip of the corsage pin, then gently remove the rubber stamp from the surface of the soap. Using a small paring knife, trim the edges of the stamped area if necessary.

Lemon Bars

This cheery lemon-yellow salt scrub bar gently buffs the skin. The white layer moisturizes with shea butter, leaving your skin feeling soft and clean, but not dry. Fine-grain sea salt ensures that this bar won't scratch the skin. Yields four to six bars, depending on size.

MATERIALS

Turmeric powder	⅛ teaspoon (.6 ml)
Gold mica powder	½ teaspoon (2.5 ml)
Lemon essential oil	1½ teaspoons (7.5 ml)
Fine-grain sea salt	2 tablespoons (30 ml)
Shea butter melt-and-pour soap	1 lb. (454 g)
Clear glycerin melt-and-pour soap	2 lbs. (908 g)

TOOLS

- Double boiler with lid
- Dough cutter
- Glass measuring cups: 4-cup (960 ml) (2)
- Knife: large
- Measuring spoons
- Metal spoon for stirring
- Mold: plastic drawer organizer, 9 × 6 × 2 inches (22 × 15.2 × 5.1 cm)
- Plastic wrap
- Rubber spatula
- Spray bottle filled with rubbing alcohol

INSTRUCTIONS

1 Using the large knife, cut the clear glycerin soap into cubes, then melt the soap in the double boiler, covering the double boiler with the lid.

2 Once the soap is melted, remove the double boiler from the heat. Stir in the turmeric and gold mica powders, then pour the soap into a glass measuring cup using the rubber spatula. Add 1 tablespoon (15 ml) of the sea salt, stirring gently to incorporate. Stir in the essential oil.

3 Using the large knife, cut the shea butter soap into cubes, then place the cubes in the glass measuring cup. Cover the cup with plastic wrap, then melt the soap in a microwave.

4 Pour the shea butter soap into the mold about one-third full, then spray the surface of the soap with rubbing alcohol to eliminate any bubbles. Allow a thin skin to form on top of the shea butter soap, then pour the colored glycerin soap into the mold. Spray the surface of the soap with rubbing alcohol. Sprinkle the surface of the soap with the sea salt. *Note:* To ensure an even layer of sea salt on top of the soap, sprinkle the sea salt using a salt shaker.

5 Allow the soap to cool and fully harden. Remove the soap from the mold, then cut it into bars using the dough cutter.

CHAPTER 4

Luxuriate

One of the least expensive, yet most pleasurable little luxuries is beautiful soap. In the guest bathroom, pretty soap makes friends and family feel cherished. In the kitchen, it turns everyday chores into more enjoyable experiences. In the master bathroom, these mini frills serve as a way to escape the pressures of life.

The soaps in this chapter have two things in common: They are beautiful and they smell terrific. Bright-green lemongrass is sure to stimulate the senses, gold and copper layers are perfect for the men in your life, pink peppermint swirls leave you tingly clean, and fresh tangerine will remind you of lazy summer days.

Black Grapefruit

This striking layered soap has a clean, uplifting scent sure to brighten your day. Thyme and pink grapefruit essential oils have astringent properties, making this soap a good choice for oily or combination skin. Black and merlot mica powders give the soap its rich color. Yields two oversize bars.

TOOLS

- Double boiler with lid
- Glass measuring cups: 4-cup (960 ml) (2)
- Knife: large
- Measuring spoons
- Metal spoons for stirring (2)
- Soap molds: oval
- Spray bottle filled with rubbing alcohol

MATERIALS

Black mica powder	⅛ teaspoon (.6 ml) plus one pinch
Merlot mica powder	½ teaspoon (2.5 ml)
Thyme essential oil	½ teaspoon (2.5 ml)
Jojoba oil	1 teaspoon (5 ml)
Pink grapefruit essential oil	1½ teaspoons (7.5 ml)
Clear glycerin melt-and-pour soap	1 lb. (454 g)

INSTRUCTIONS

1 Using the large knife, cut the soap into cubes, then melt the soap in the double boiler, covering the double boiler with the lid.

2 Once the soap is melted, remove the double boiler from the heat. Stir in the jojoba oil then pour one-third of the soap into one glass measuring cup and two-thirds into the remaining cup.

3 Into the measuring cup with less soap, add ⅛ teaspoon (.6 ml) black mica powder, stirring gently to incorporate.

4 Into the remaining measuring cup, add the pinch of black mica powder and the merlot mica powder, stirring gently to incorporate. Stir in the essential oils.

5 Pour the merlot soap into the molds, filling the molds about two-thirds full. Spray the surface of the soap with rubbing alcohol to eliminate any bubbles. Let a thin skin form on the soap, spray the surface of the soap with rubbing alcohol again (this ensures the layers will not separate), then fill the molds with the black soap. Spray the surface of the soap with rubbing alcohol.

6 Allow the soap to cool and fully harden, then remove the soap from the molds.

Energizing Lemongrass

Lemongrass essential oil is known for its ability to reduce stress and brighten the mood. A mixture of chlorophyll and turmeric powders gives this soap its show-stopping color. Dried lemongrass is gently exfoliating and gives a natural look to the soap. Yields approximately eight bars.

MATERIALS

Bergamot essential oil	¼ teaspoon (1.25 ml)
Lemongrass essential oil	1 teaspoon (5 ml)
Turmeric powder	1 teaspoon (5 ml)
Dried lemongrass	2 teaspoons (10 ml)
Chlorophyll powder	1 gel capsule
Shea butter melt-and-pour suspension soap	1 lb. (454 g)

TOOLS

- Double boiler with lid
- Glass measuring cup: 4-cup (960 ml)
- Knife: large
- Measuring spoons
- Metal spoon for stirring
- Plastic candy molds: dessert shells
- Rubber spatula
- Spray bottle filled with rubbing alcohol

INSTRUCTIONS

1 Using the large knife, cut the soap into cubes, then melt the soap in the double boiler, covering the double boiler with the lid.

2 Once the soap is melted, remove the double boiler from the heat. Open the chlorophyll powder gel capsule, add ⅛ teaspoon (.6 ml) of the powder to the soap, stirring gently to incorporate. Stir in the turmeric powder and dried lemongrass.

3 Transfer the soap into the glass measuring cup using the rubber spatula, stir in the essential oils, then pour the soap into the molds. Spray the surface of the soap with rubbing alcohol to eliminate any bubbles.

4 Allow the soap to cool and fully harden, then remove the soap from the molds.

Orange Marmalade

Tone-on-tone coloring is the secret to creating this decorative soap. Turmeric powder adds just the right amount of yellow to create the perfect orange color. Consider making the soap curls ahead of time so the bars are quicker to complete. Yields approximately four to six bars.

MATERIALS

Sweet orange essential oil	1 teaspoon (5 ml)
Turmeric powder	2 teaspoons (10 ml)
Orange mica powder	1 tablespoon (15 ml)
Olive oil melt-and-pour suspension soap	1¼ lbs. (567 g)

TOOLS

- Candy thermometer
- Double boiler with lid
- Glass measuring cups: 4-cup (960 ml) (2)
- Knife: large
- Measuring spoons
- Metal spoon
- Paring knife or vegetable peeler
- Plastic container with lid
- Plastic wrap
- Soap molds: rectangle
- Spray bottle filled with rubbing alcohol

INSTRUCTIONS

1. Using the large knife, cut the soap into cubes. Melt ¼ lb. (114 g) of soap in a glass measuring cup in a microwave, covering the cup with plastic wrap before melting the soap.

2. Once the soap is melted, add 1 teaspoon (5 ml) turmeric powder and 2 teaspoons (10 ml) orange mica powder, stirring gently to incorporate. Pour the soap into a soap mold, then spray the surface of the soap with rubbing alcohol to eliminate any bubbles. Allow the soap to cool and fully harden, then remove the soap from the mold.

3. Using the paring knife or vegetable peeler, make soap curls from the finished bar of soap (see page 20). Put the soap curls into the plastic container, then put the container in the refrigerator for 15 minutes.

4. Melt the remaining 1 lb. (454 g) of soap in the double boiler, covering the double boiler with the lid. As the soap is melting, add the soap curls to the molds.

5. Once the soap is melted, remove the double boiler from the heat. Add 1 teaspoon (5 ml) orange mica powder and 1 teaspoon (5 ml) turmeric powder, stirring gently to incorporate. Pour the soap into the second measuring cup, then stir in the essential oil. Gently stir the soap for a few minutes to allow it to cool to 110° F (43.3° C).

6. Spray the soap curls in the molds with rubbing alcohol to prevent air pockets and bubbles, then slowly pour the melted soap over the soap curls. Spray the surface of the soap with rubbing alcohol to eliminate any bubbles.

7. Allow the soap to cool and fully harden, then remove the soap from the molds.

Spicy Stripes

This unique layered bar features a warm, masculine scent. Made using clear glycerin soap, it imparts a clean feel without drying the skin. The layers are surprisingly easy to create—simply tilt the mold between pouring the different colors of soap. Yields one bar.

MATERIALS

Patchouli essential oil	⅛ teaspoon (.6 ml)
Coral mica powder	¼ teaspoon (1.25 ml)
Gold mica powder	¼ teaspoon (1.25 ml)
Lavender essential oil	¼ teaspoon (1.25 ml)
Ylang-ylang essential oil	1 teaspoon (5 ml)
Sandalwood essential oil	1¼ teaspoons (6.25 ml)
Clear glycerin melt-and-pour soap	1 lb. (454 g)

TOOLS

- Double boiler with lid
- Glass measuring cups: 4-cup (960 ml) (2)
- Knife: large
- Measuring spoons
- Metal spoons for stirring (2)
- Mold: plastic drawer organizer, 3 x 3 x 2 inches (7.6 x 7.6 x 5.1 cm)
- Spray bottle filled with rubbing alcohol
- Wooden chopsticks or other small, stackable item

INSTRUCTIONS

1. Using the large knife, cut the soap into cubes, then melt the soap in the double boiler, covering the double boiler with the lid.

2. Once the soap is melted, remove the double boiler from the heat, then stir in the essential oils. Pour half of the melted soap into each of the measuring cups.

3. Stir the coral mica powder into one of the measuring cups. Stir the gold mica powder into the remaining measuring cup.

4. Place the bottom of one side of the mold on a wooden chopstick, pour a small amount of the coral-colored soap in the mold, then spray the top of the soap with rubbing alcohol to eliminate any bubbles. Let a thin skin form on top of the soap, then spray the surface of the soap with rubbing alcohol (this ensures that the layers will stick together). Remove the chopstick. Place two chopsticks on top of each other, then place the chopsticks under the opposite bottom edge of the mold. Pour a small amount of gold-colored soap in the mold, then spray the top of the soap with rubbing alcohol.

5. Repeat Step 4, altering the height and placement of the chopsticks, until the mold is filled. *Note:* Reheat the soap in the measuring cups as needed during this process.

6. Allow the soap to cool and fully harden, then remove the soap from the mold.

Peppermint Tingle

Peppermint rejuvenates the skin and awakens the senses as it cleans. This pretty swirled soap is a refreshing way to start your day or to give yourself a jump start before an evening out. Peppermint essential oil is regarded for its ability to improve concentration and mental accuracy. Yields approximately four bars.

MATERIALS

Red mica powder, divided	1⅛ teaspoons (6.25 ml)
Peppermint essential oil, divided in half	2 teaspoons (10 ml)
Shea butter melt-and-pour suspension soap	1 lb. (454 g)

TOOLS

- Double boiler with lid
- Dough cutter
- Glass measuring cups: 4-cup (960 ml) (2)
- Knife: large
- Measuring spoons
- Metal spoons for stirring (2)
- Mold: plastic drawer organizer, 9 × 6 × 2 inches (22 × 15.2 × 5.1 cm)
- Plastic wrap
- Spray bottle filled with rubbing alcohol

INSTRUCTIONS

1 Using the large knife, cut the soap into cubes, then melt the soap in the double boiler, covering the double boiler with the lid.

2 Once the soap is melted, remove the double boiler from the heat. Stir in the essential oil, then pour half of the melted soap into each of the measuring cups.

3 To one measuring cup, add ⅛ teaspoon (.6 ml) mica powder, stirring gently to incorporate. Cover the measuring cup with plastic wrap.

4 In the remaining measuring cup, add 1 teaspoon (5 ml) mica powder, stirring gently to incorporate.

5 Remove the plastic wrap from the first measuring cup, then pour the colored soaps side by side into the mold. Spray the surface of the soap with rubbing alcohol to eliminate any bubbles, then swirl the two colors together (see page 19). Spray the surface of the soap with rubbing alcohol again.

6 Allow the soap to cool and fully harden, then remove the soap from the mold. Cut the soap into bars using the dough cutter.

Tropical Dream

The smell of virgin coconut oil and fruity essential oils will have you dreaming of a tropical escape. Olive and coconut oils make this layered soap extra moisturizing. The yellow-orange color is achieved with arnica seed-infused olive oil. This is a great soap for very dry skin. Yields six to eight bars, depending on size.

MATERIALS

Turmeric powder	¼ teaspoon (1.25 ml)
Ylang-ylang essential oil	¼ teaspoon (1.25 ml)
Tangerine essential oil	½ teaspoon (2.5 ml)
Pink grapefruit essential oil	1 teaspoon (5 ml)
Arnica seed-infused olive oil	2 teaspoons (10 ml)
Vanilla essential oil, divided in half	2 teaspoons (10 ml)
Virgin coconut oil	1 tablespoon (15 ml)
Clear glycerin melt-and-pour soap	¾ lb. (342 g)
Shea butter melt-and-pour soap	1½ lbs. (682 g)

TOOLS

- Double boiler with lid
- Dough cutter
- Glass measuring cup: 4-cup (960 ml)
- Knife: large
- Measuring spoons
- Metal spoons for stirring
- Mold: plastic drawer organizer, 9 × 3 × 2 inches (22 × 7.6 × 5.1 cm)
- Plastic wrap
- Rubber spatula
- Spray bottle filled with rubbing alcohol

INSTRUCTIONS

1 Using the large knife, cut the clear glycerin soap into cubes, then melt the soap in the double boiler, covering the double boiler with the lid.

2 Once the soap is melted, remove the double boiler from the heat. Stir in the olive oil and turmeric powder, then transfer the soap into a glass measuring cup using the rubber spatula. Stir in the pink grapefruit, tangerine, and ylang-ylang essential oils and 1 teaspoon (5 ml) of the vanilla essential oil. Cover the measuring cup with plastic wrap.

3 Using the large knife, cut the shea butter soap into cubes, then melt the soap in the double boiler, covering the double boiler with the lid.

4 Once the soap is melted, remove the double boiler from the heat. Stir in the virgin coconut oil and 1 teaspoon (5 ml) of the vanilla essential oil. Pour the soap into the mold, filling it one-third full. Spray the surface with rubbing alcohol to eliminate any bubbles.

5 Allow a thin skin to form on top of the soap in the mold, spray the surface of the soap with rubbing alcohol, then pour the colored glycerin soap into the mold, filling the mold two-thirds full. Spray the surface of the soap with rubbing alcohol to eliminate any bubbles.

6 Allow a thin skin to form on top of the soap in the mold, spray the surface of the soap with rubbing alcohol, then pour the remainder of the shea butter into the mold, filling the mold. Spray the surface of the soap with rubbing alcohol to eliminate any bubbles.

7 Allow the soap the cool and fully harden. Remove the soap from the mold, then cut it into bars using the dough cutter.

Ebony and Ivory

The colors and shape of these soaps represent the yin and yang of life; though things may appear to be different from one another, everything is all part of an interdependent, greater whole. The soap is scented with warm, calming essential oils and is moisturizing to the skin. Yields approximately four bars.

MATERIALS

Clove bud essential oil	¼ teaspoon (1.25 ml)
Lavender essential oil	¼ teaspoon (1.25 ml)
Black luster mica powder	½ teaspoon (2.5 ml)
Patchouli essential oil	½ teaspoon (2.5 ml)
Titanium dioxide	1 teaspoon (5 ml)
Ylang-ylang essential oil	1 teaspoon (5 ml)
Clear glycerin melt-and-pour soap	2 lbs. (908 g)

TOOLS

- Candy thermometer
- Cutting board or cookie sheet
- Double boiler with lid
- Glass measuring cups: 4-cup (960 ml) (3)
- Knife: large
- Measuring spoons
- Metal spoons for stirring (2)
- Molds: PVC pipe, 3 × 3 inch (7.6 × 7.6 cm) (2)
- Plastic wrap
- Rubber bands
- Spray bottle filled with rubbing alcohol
- Wavy cutter or dough cutter

INSTRUCTIONS

1 Using the plastic wrap and rubber bands, prepare the PVC pipe molds for use (see page 17). Set the molds on a flat, even surface.

2 Using the large knife, cut the soap into cubes, then melt the soap in the double boiler, covering the double boiler with the lid.

3 Once the soap is melted, remove the double boiler from the heat. Stir in the essential oils, then pour even amounts of the melted soap into each of the measuring cups. Cover one measuring cup with plastic wrap and set aside.

4 Add the black luster mica powder to one of the remaining measuring cups, stirring gently to incorporate. This soap will now be a pearlescent black.

5 Add the titanium dioxide to the remaining measuring cup, stirring to incorporate. This soap will now be bright white.

6 Pour the black soap into one of the PVC molds, and the white soap into the other PVC mold. Allow the soap to cool and fully harden, then remove the soap from the molds.

continued

7   Using the wavy cutter or dough cutter, cut the soaps lengthwise into various size pieces. Put the soap pieces into the molds, alternating colors and leaving a small amount of space between each piece. Put the molds on a flat surface, such as a small cutting board or cookie sheet, then place the molds in a refrigerator for 15 minutes.

8   Remove the soaps from the refrigerator, adjusting the soap pieces in the molds if necessary (they may shift when moved to and from the refrigerator), then spray them generously with rubbing alcohol to prevent any air bubbles and ensure that the layers will stick together.

9   Reheat the uncolored soap in the microwave, then let it cool to about 110° F (43.3° C). Pour the soap over the colored soap in the molds, then spray the surface of the soap with rubbing alcohol.

10 Allow the soap to cool and fully harden. To cut, push half of the soap out of one of the molds then cut the soap with the wavy or dough cutter. Repeat with second mold.

Carved Quartz

The neutral colors and interesting shape of this soap take a little time and patience to achieve, but the results are worth it. You can create colored gems using various shades of purple (for amethyst) or green (for emeralds). An Internet search will provide pictures of different gems to inspire you and guide you in your carving efforts. Yields up to eight bars, depending on size.

MATERIALS

Gold mica powder	▪	⅛ teaspoon (.6 ml)
Lime essential oil	▪	⅛ teaspoon (.6 ml)
Nutmeg	▪	¼ teaspoon (1.25 ml)
Tangerine essential oil	▪	¼ teaspoon (1.25 ml)
Pink grapefruit essential oil	▪	1 teaspoon (5 ml)
Shea butter melt-and-pour soap	▪	⅛ lb. (57 g)
Clear glycerin melt-and-pour soap, divided	▪	2 lbs. (908 g)

TOOLS

- Coins, plastic caps, or other small items: for lifting edges of mold during layering process
- Double boiler with lid
- Dough cutter
- Glass measuring cups: 4-cup (960 ml) (4)
- Knives: large and paring
- Measuring spoons
- Metal spoons for stirring (4)
- Mold: plastic drawer organizer, 9 × 3 × 2 inches (22 × 7.6 × 5.1 cm)
- Plastic wrap
- Spray bottle filled with rubbing alcohol

INSTRUCTIONS

1 Using the large knife, cut the clear glycerin soap into cubes, then melt 1¾ lbs. (796 g) of the soap in the double boiler, covering the double boiler with the lid.

2 Once the soap is melted, remove the double boiler from the heat. Let the soap cool for a couple of minutes then stir in the essential oils.

3 Pour equal amounts of the soap into two glass measuring cups. Add the nutmeg to one of the measuring cups, stirring gently to incorporate. The second cup of soap will now be referred to as the plain, scented soap.

4 Add ¼ lb. (114 g) clear glycerin soap to an empty measuring cup, then melt the soap in the microwave, covering the measuring cup with plastic wrap before melting the soap.

5 Using the large knife, cut the shea butter soap into cubes, then place the cubes in the remaining glass measuring cup. Cover the glass measuring cup with plastic wrap, then melt the soap in a microwave.

6 Line up the cups of melted soap on your work surface. *Note:* The soaps need to be about the same temperature before they are poured into the mold. Warm the soaps in the microwave in 10-second intervals until they are evenly warmed.

7 Using the same method used to create the Spicy Stripes soap (page 80), layer the plain, scented soap, the scented soap with nutmeg, and the shea butter soap in the mold. Use the coins or other small, stackable items to vary the height of the sides of mold between layers. Sprinkle the gold mica powder on top of the various layers to give a speckled effect to the soap.

8 Pour the clear, unscented soap as the last layer. Allow the soap to cool and fully harden, then remove the soap from the mold.

9 Using the dough cutter, cut the soap in half lengthwise, then cut it in half widthwise. Using the paring knife, carve the soap into natural quartz shapes.

Soap Success

When creating layered or swirled soaps, be sure to use clean spoons when making the different colors of soap. This will prevent unwanted color accidents.

Simply Lavender

Perhaps the easiest recipe in this book, the Simply Lavender soap is perfect for the first-time soap maker. Dried lavender flowers look like little pods when added to soap. If you prefer a more textured look, crush the flowers using a mortar and pestle. Gently crushing the flowers also releases fragrance and will make the soaps more heavily scented. Yields six bars.

TOOLS

- Double boiler with lid
- Glass measuring cup: 4-cup (960 ml)
- Knife: large
- Measuring spoons
- Metal spoon for stirring
- Mold: silicone muffin pan
- Rubber spatula
- Spray bottle filled with rubbing alcohol

MATERIALS

Lavender essential oil	1 teaspoon (5 ml)
Dried lavender flowers	2 teaspoons (10 ml)
Olive oil melt-and-pour suspension soap	1 lb. (454 g)

INSTRUCTIONS

1 Using the large knife, cut the soap into cubes, then melt the soap in the double boiler, covering the double boiler with the lid. Once the soap is melted, remove the double boiler from the heat. Add the dried lavender flowers, stirring gently to incorporate.

2 Transfer the soap into the glass measuring cup using the rubber spatula, stir in the essential oil, then pour the soap into the molds. Spray the surface of the soap with rubbing alcohol to eliminate any bubbles.

3 Allow the soap to cool and fully harden, then remove the soap from the molds.

CHAPTER 5

Good, Clean, Fun

Getting clean is serious business, but it should never be a chore. Amusing shapes, embedded treats, and dessert-inspired soaps put a smile on even the grumpiest member of your household. These soaps are cute enough to leave on display and prove that natural soaps are anything but boring.

The projects in this chapter make cleaning up fun. These soaps don't exfoliate or target special skin concerns; they simply cleanse the skin. Using easy-to-find pans and molds, you will learn to make soaps that enhance the happiness quotient. Get kids excited to lather up with fun shapes and colors, and celebrate a special birthday or graduation with cupcake soaps—complete with frosting and sugar sprinkles. Invite friends over for tea and send them home with a great-smelling bundt cake soap, or make one-of-a-kind wedding favors.

Building Blocks

These fun soaps were made using silicone cake pans and ice cube trays. The small soaps are the perfect size for little hands while the large soaps are great for use in the bathtub. This recipe does not call for an essential oil, but if you prefer fragranced soaps, use a scent kids will love such as coconut, lemon, orange, or vanilla. Yields approximately two large and 16 small bars.

MATERIALS

Turmeric powder	½ teaspoon (2.5 ml)
Kelp powder	1 gel capsule
Cucumber olive oil melt-and-pour soap	2 lbs. (908 g)

TOOLS

- Double boiler with lid
- Glass measuring cups: 4-cup (960 ml) (2)
- Knife: large
- Measuring spoons
- Molds: silicone cake pans and ice cube trays, building blocks shapes
- Spray bottle filled with rubbing alcohol

INSTRUCTIONS

1 Using the large knife, cut the soap into cubes, then melt the soap in the double boiler, covering the double boiler with the lid.

2 Once the soap is melted, remove the double boiler from the heat, then pour equal amounts of the soap into each measuring cup.

3 Stir the turmeric powder into one measuring cup a bit at a time until the desired color is reached.

4 Open the kelp powder gel capsule and stir the powder into the remaining measuring cup a bit at a time until the desired color is reached.

5 Pour the soap into the molds, then spray the surface of the soap with rubbing alcohol to eliminate any bubbles.

6 Allow the soap to cool and fully harden, then remove the soap from the molds.

Fruity Cupcakes

Made with kid-friendly scents and colors, these cute cupcakes would be great party favors. Buttermilk ensures a smooth lather. The sugar sprinkled on top of the soaps will melt once the soap is wet. Yields approximately six cupcake soaps.

MATERIALS

Curry powder	¼ teaspoon (1.25 ml)
Green mica powder	¼ teaspoon (1.25 ml)
Pink mica powder	¼ teaspoon (1.25 ml)
Lemon essential oil	1 teaspoon (5 ml)
Melon essential oil	1 teaspoon (5 ml)
Pink grapefruit essential oil	1 teaspoon (5 ml)
Vanilla essential oil	1 teaspoon (5 ml)
Buttermilk powder	1 tablespoon (15 ml)
Hot water	1 tablespoon (15 ml)
Colored sugar	2 tablespoons (30 ml)
Shea butter melt-and-pour soap	¼ lb. (114 g)
Clear glycerin melt-and-pour soap	1 lb. (454 g)

TOOLS

- Bowls: small (2)
- Double boiler with lid
- Electric mixer with whisk
- Glass measuring cups: 4-cup (960 ml) (4)
- Knife: large
- Measuring spoons
- Metal spoons for stirring (4)
- Molds: silicone cupcake molds (6)
- Parchment paper
- Plastic wrap
- Spray bottle filled with rubbing alcohol
- Strainer or cheesecloth

INSTRUCTIONS

1 Using the large knife, cut the clear glycerin soap into cubes, then melt the soap in the double boiler, covering the double boiler with the lid.

2 As the clear glycerin soap is melting, use the large knife to cut the shea butter soap into cubes. Place the cubes in a measuring cup, then melt the soap in the microwave, covering the soap with plastic wrap prior to melting.

3 Mix the buttermilk powder and hot water in a small bowl. Using a separate bowl and a strainer or cheesecloth, strain the mixture to remove any lumps. Once the shea butter soap is melted, add the buttermilk mixture, stirring to incorporate. Stir in the vanilla essential oil. Cover the measuring cup with plastic wrap.

4 Once the clear glycerin soap has melted, remove the double boiler from the heat, then divide the soap equally into three glass measuring cups.

5 To one of the measuring cups, add the curry powder, stirring gently to incorporate. Stir in the lemon essential oil; cover the measuring cup with plastic wrap.

6 To another of the measuring cups, add the green mica powder, stirring gently to incorporate. Stir in the melon essential oil; cover the measuring cup with plastic wrap.

continued

7 To the remaining measuring cup, add the pink mica powder, stirring gently to incorporate. Stir in the pink grapefruit essential oil; cover the measuring cup with plastic wrap.

8 Working one color at a time, pour the glycerin soap into the cupcake molds. *Note:* Use one color of soap in each mold. Spray the surface of the soap with rubbing alcohol to eliminate any bubbles.

9 Reheat the shea butter soap in the microwave, then whip the soap using the electric mixer until it begins to thicken. Quickly spray the surface of the cupcake soaps with rubbing alcohol then pour or spoon the shea butter mixture on top of the cupcakes. Immediately sprinkle the top of the soaps with the colored sugar.

10 Allow the cupcake soaps to cool and fully harden, then remove the soaps from the molds.

Truly Yours

The perfect symbol of love, these heart-shaped soaps will gladden the heart of every recipient. The soaps are gently scented and great for Valentine's Day gifts or to tuck into gift baskets for weddings or bridal showers. Yields four soaps, two of each color.

MATERIALS

Neroli essential oil	¼ teaspoon (1.25 ml)
Red mica powder	¼ teaspoon (1.25 ml)
Rose essential oil	1 teaspoon (5 ml)
Clear glycerin melt-and-pour soap	½ lb. (227 g)
Shea butter melt-and-pour soap	½ lb. (227 g)

TOOLS

- Cookie cutter: metal heart-shape, smaller diameter than heart shapes of muffin pan
- Double boiler with lid
- Dough cutter
- Glass measuring cups: 4-cup (960 ml) (2)
- Knife: large
- Measuring spoons
- Metal spoons for stirring (2)
- Mold: silicone muffin pan with heart-shaped cups
- Plastic wrap
- Rubber spatula
- Spray bottle filled with rubbing alcohol

INSTRUCTIONS

1   Using the large knife, cut the shea butter soap into cubes, then place the cubes in the glass measuring cup. Cover the glass measuring cup with plastic wrap, then melt the soap in a microwave.

2   Remove the measuring cup from the microwave, pour the soap into the mold completely filling the heart cups, then spray the surface of the soap with rubbing alcohol to eliminate any bubbles. *Note:* Each soap color will fill approximately two heart cups in the muffin pan.

3   Using the large knife, cut the clear glycerin soap into cubes, then melt the soap in the double boiler, covering the double boiler with the lid.

4   Once the soap is melted, remove the double boiler from the heat. Add the mica powder, stirring gently to incorporate. Stir in the essential oils. Transfer the soap into a glass measuring cup using the rubber spatula, then pour the soap into the empty heart cups in the muffin pan. Make sure the heart cups are completely filled. Spray the surface of the soap with rubbing alcohol. Allow the soap to cool and fully harden, then remove the soap hearts from the muffin pan.

5 Using the cookie cutter, cut out a heart shape from the center of each piece of soap.

6 Using the measuring cups, melt the small heart shapes (one color in each measuring cup) in the microwave, then let the soap cool for a couple of minutes.

7 Place the large hearts back in the muffin pan. Pour the melted red soap into the center of the white heart-shaped soaps. Pour the melted shea butter soap into the center of the red heart-shaped soaps.

8 Allow the heart soaps to cool and fully harden, then remove from the muffin pan. If necessary, trim the back of the soaps using the dough cutter.

A Day at the Beach

These pretty shell soaps are an easy way to dress up a bathroom. Whip up a bunch before hosting a party to make your guests feel special. Tea tree essential oil is a natural antiseptic, ensuring clean hands. Yields approximately eight small soaps.

MATERIALS

Blue-green mica powder	⅛ teaspoon (.6 ml)
Cedarwood essential oil	⅛ teaspoon (.6 ml)
Tea tree essential oil	⅛ teaspoon (.6 ml)
Eucalyptus essential oil	¼ teaspoon (1.25 ml)
Clear glycerin melt-and-pour soap	¼ lb. (114 g)
Shea butter melt-and-pour suspension soap	¼ lb. (114 g)

TOOLS

- Glass measuring cups: 4-cup (960 ml) (2)
- Knife: large
- Measuring spoons
- Metal spoons for stirring (2)
- Plastic wrap
- Rubber spatula
- Soap molds: seashells
- Spray bottle filled with rubbing alcohol
- Toothpicks

INSTRUCTIONS

1 Using the large knife, cut the glycerin soap into cubes, then place the cubes in one of the glass measuring cups. Cover the glass measuring cup with plastic wrap, then melt the soap in a microwave. Repeat with the shea butter soap.

2 Stir the essential oils and mica powder into the clear glycerin soap. Pour an even amount of the colored soap into the molds, then pour the shea butter soap on top. Using the toothpicks, swirl the soap in the molds. Spray the surface of the soap with rubbing alcohol to eliminate any bubbles.

3 Allow the soap to cool and fully harden, then remove the soap from the molds.

Wedding Favors

Create unique keepsakes for your wedding guests with this simple recipe. Use mica powders or natural herbs to make soap that matches your personal theme. Shea butter soap can be used on all skin types. Yields approximately 16 mini soaps.

MATERIALS

Sandalwood essential oil	½ teaspoon (2.5 ml)
Sweet orange essential oil	1 teaspoon (5 ml)
Chlorophyll powder	1 gel capsule
Kelp powder	2 gel capsules
Shea butter melt-and-pour suspension soap	1 lb. (454 g)

TOOLS

- Double boiler with lid
- Glass measuring cups: 4-cup (960 ml) (2)
- Knife: large
- Measuring spoons
- Metal spoons for stirring (2)
- Mold: non-stick mini muffin pan with multiple cups
- Plastic wrap
- Spray bottle filled with rubbing alcohol

INSTRUCTIONS

1. Using the large knife, cut the soap into cubes, then melt the soap in the double boiler, covering the double boiler with the lid.

2. Once the soap is melted, remove the double boiler from the heat, then pour half of the melted soap into each of the measuring cups. Cover one measuring cup with plastic wrap. Set aside.

3. Open the kelp powder gel capsules, then add the powder to the soap in the remaining measuring cup, stirring gently to incorporate. Open the chlorophyll powder gel capsule, then stir in a pinch of the powder. Stir in the essential oils.

4. Reheat the uncolored soap in the microwave in 10-second intervals, until melted.

5. Layer the soap in the mini muffin pan (see page 19), then spray the surface of the soap with rubbing alcohol to eliminate any bubbles.

6. Allow the soap to cool and fully harden, then remove the soap from the molds.

Mini Bundt Cakes

These orange bundt cakes are drizzled with icing. They smell good enough to eat so you will want to keep an eye on little ones to make sure they don't wash their mouths out with soap. Buttermilk powder and coconut oil soften and moisturize, making this a great soap for dry skin. Yields approximately four mini bundt cake soaps.

MATERIALS

Coconut oil	½ teaspoon (2.5 ml)
Vanilla essential oil, divided	1½ teaspoons (7.5 ml)
Arnica-seed infused olive oil	2 teaspoons (10 ml)
Sweet orange essential oil	2 teaspoons (10 ml)
Buttermilk powder	2 tablespoons (30 ml)
Hot water	2 tablespoons (30 ml)
Shea butter melt-and-pour soap	1¼ lbs. (568 g)

TOOLS

- Bowls: small (2)
- Double boiler with lid
- Glass measuring cups: 4-cup (960 ml) (2)
- Knives: large and paring
- Measuring spoons
- Metal spoon for stirring
- Mold: non-stick mini bundt cake pan with multiple openings
- Parchment paper
- Plastic wrap
- Rubber spatula
- Spray bottle filled with rubbing alcohol
- Strainer or cheesecloth

INSTRUCTIONS

1 Using the large knife, cut the soap into cubes. Melt 1 lb. (454 g) of the soap in the double boiler, covering the double boiler with the lid.

2 As the soap is melting, mix the buttermilk powder and the hot water in a small bowl. Using a separate bowl and a strainer or cheesecloth, strain the mixture to remove any lumps.

3 Once the soap is melted, remove the double boiler from the heat, then add the buttermilk mixture, stirring gently to incorporate.

4 Transfer the soap into a glass measuring cup using the rubber spatula, then stir in the infused olive oil, sweet orange essential oil, and 1 teaspoon (5 ml) vanilla essential oil. Pour the soap into the mold, then spray the surface of the soap with rubbing alcohol to eliminate any bubbles.

5 Allow the soap to cool and fully harden, then remove the soap from the mold. Place the soaps on parchment paper.

6 Place ¼ lb. (114 g) of the soap into the second glass measuring cup, then melt the soap in the microwave, covering the measuring cup with plastic wrap before melting the soap. Once the soap is melted, stir in the coconut oil and ½ teaspoon (2.5 ml) vanilla essential oil.

7 Spray the surface of the bundt cake soaps with rubbing alcohol (this ensures that the layers will stick together), then drizzle the remaining melted soap over the bundt cake soaps so they look like they are frosted. Allow the soap to cool and fully harden. Using the paring knife, trim the "frosting" as needed. Smooth the edges of the trimmed soap with your fingers.

Just Ducky

Make taking a bath fun for kids by embedding small treats in their soaps. This method can be used with any type of mold and small rubber toy. Because the toys are small, children 3 years and younger shouldn't use this soap without close supervision. Yields approximately one bar.

MATERIALS

Blue mica powder	⅛ teaspoon (.6 ml)
Rubber ducky or other toy to embed	1 small
Clear glycerin melt-and-pour soap, divided	1 lb. (454 g)

TOOLS

- Glass measuring cups: 4-cup (960 ml) (2)
- Knife: large
- Measuring spoons
- Metal spoons for stirring (2)
- Mold: round PVC pipe 3 × 3 inches (7.6 × 7.6 cm)
- Plastic wrap
- Rubber bands
- Rubber spatula
- Spray bottle filled with rubbing alcohol

INSTRUCTIONS

1 Using the plastic wrap and rubber bands, prepare the mold for use (see page 17).

2 Using the large knife, cut the glycerin soap into cubes. Put ¼ lb. (114 g) of the soap into a glass measuring cup, then melt the soap in a microwave, covering the cup with plastic wrap before melting the soap.

3 Once the soap is melted, stir in the mica powder. Cover the measuring cup with plastic wrap and set aside.

4 Place the remaining soap into the second glass measuring cup, then melt the soap in a microwave, covering the measuring cup with plastic wrap before melting the soap.

5 Pour the colored soap into the mold. Wait for a thin skin to form on top of the soap, remove the skin, then place the toy in the soap. Spray the surface of the soap with rubbing alcohol to eliminate any bubbles. *Note:* You may need to hold the toy in place until the soap begins to harden.

6 Pour the clear glycerin soap into the mold. Allow the soap to cool and fully harden, then remove the soap from the mold.

Cookie Cutter Shapes

If you have a hard time finding molds you like, cookie cutters may fill the bill. Let your kids get in on the action by having them cut out the shapes. Beeswax was added to this recipe to harden the soap, making the bars last longer. Yields approximately four soaps, depending on the size of the cookie cutters.

MATERIALS

Jasmine essential oil	1 teaspoon (5 ml)
Vanilla essential oil	1 teaspoon (5 ml)
Beeswax: grated	2 tablespoons (30 ml)
Buttermilk powder	2 tablespoons (30 ml)
Hot water	2 tablespoons (30 ml)
Shea butter melt-and-pour suspension soap	2 lbs. (908 g)

TOOLS

Bowls: small (2)

Double boiler with lid

Glass measuring cup: 4-cup (960 ml)

Knife: large

Measuring spoons

Metal cookie cutters

Metal spoon for stirring

Mold: square cake pan

Rubber spatula

Spray bottle filled with rubbing alcohol

Strainer or cheesecloth

INSTRUCTIONS

1 Using the large knife, cut the soap into cubes, then melt the soap in the double boiler, covering the double boiler with the lid.

2 As the soap is melting, mix the buttermilk powder with hot water in a small bowl. Using a separate bowl and a strainer or cheesecloth, strain the mixture to remove any lumps.

3 Once the soap is melted, remove the double boiler from the heat. Add the grated beeswax, stirring gently until it melts. Stir in the buttermilk mixture.

4 Transfer the soap into the glass measuring cup using the rubber spatula, then stir in the essential oils. Pour the soap into the mold, then spray the surface of the soap with rubbing alcohol to eliminate any bubbles.

5 Allow the soap to cool and fully harden, then remove the soap from the mold. Using the cookie cutters, cut shapes from the soap.

CHAPTER 6

Wrap It Up

Handmade soap is a gift from the heart. Taking time to create pretty packages will make your soaps even more special. To prevent soap from hardening, wrap your bars in plastic wrap sealed with a sticker prior to placing in bags, boxes, or dishes.

The projects in this chapter feature presentations that are easy, unique, and fun to create. Make one-of-a-kind stamped boxes, create cigar band wraps, and repurpose paper lunch bags.

Washcloth Soap Bag

A washcloth and needle and thread are all that's
needed to create this fun soap bag.

- Needle and thread
- Sewing or craft scissors

MATERIALS

- Cotton cord or ribbon: 12 inches (30.4 cm)
- Washcloth

INSTRUCTIONS

1. Place the side edges of the washcloth side by side. Using the needle and thread, sew the edges together.

2. Turn the piece inside out and fold one end down about 2 inches (5 cm). Using the needle and thread, sew a seam along the edge to form a pocket for the cord. *Note:* This is the top edge of the bag.

3. Using the needle and thread, sew the bottom edge closed.

4. Carefully cut an opening for the cord along the side seam of the pocket. Using the needle and thread, reinforce the cut edges of the seam. Thread the cord or ribbon through the pocket. Place a soap in the bag and tie the bag closed.

Bags and Tags

This is a great way to wrap soaps for party favors. Consider adding a small cuticle brush, bath scrubby, or soap dish to the bags to make them even more special.

TOOLS

- Craft glue
- Craft scissors
- Paper punches: various sizes and shapes
- Ruler

MATERIALS

- Decorative paper
- Embellishments: brads, dried flowers, stamps
- Gift bag: paper
- Optional: paper shreds
- Paper and cardboard tag shapes in various sizes and colors
- Plastic wrap
- Ribbon or raffia

INSTRUCTIONS

1 Place the soap in the bag. If you are putting paper shreds or other items into the bag, wrap the soap with plastic wrap before placing it into the bag.

2 Using the decorative paper and embellishments, decorate the gift tags. Tie the tags to the bags with ribbon or raffia or secure them with a brad.

Stamped Boxes

Many sizes and styles of boxes can easily be found at craft stores.

You could also consider repurposing boxes from purchased soaps.

These unique boxes can be decorated to fit any occasion.

- Paper towels
- Scissors

MATERIALS

- Boxes: various shapes and sizes
- Inkpads: desired colors
- Ribbon
- Rubber stamps

INSTRUCTIONS

1 Cover your work surface with paper towels. Open the box and lay it flat on the work surface. Using the inkpad and rubber stamps decorate one side of the box. Allow the ink to dry. Repeat to decorate the sides and top of the box.

2 Fold the box along the scored lines.

3 Place the soap inside the box and close the box. Tie the ribbon around the box handle, if desired.

Treasure Box

A long, thin box is an elegant way to present soaps. Use soaps
of the same shape and size for a smart presentation.

TOOLS

- Craft knife or scissors
- Paintbrush: small
- Paper piercing tool
- Round-nose pliers
- Ruler
- Self-healing cutting mat
- Wire cutter

MATERIALS

- Acrylic paint to match decorative paper
- Beads (3)
- Craft wire: 22-gauge (4 inches [10.2 cm])
- Decorative paper
- Glue stick
- Papier-mâché box

INSTRUCTIONS

1. Using the ruler or measuring tape, measure the inside of the top and bottom portions of the box. Using the measurements and a pencil, draw patterns on the back of the decorative paper and cut out the shapes with the craft scissors. Repeat for the outside of the box.

2. Using the craft glue, carefully adhere the cut pieces to the coordinating portion of the box; allow the glue to dry.

3. Using the paper piercing tool, make a hole in the middle of the top of the box.

4. Using the paintbrush and acrylic paint, cover any exposed edges of the box. Allow to dry.

5. Using the round-nose pliers, make a loop on one end of the wire. Thread the beads onto the wire, then place the straight end of the wire through the hole in the top of the box and make a loop at the end of the wire.

6. Place soaps inside the box.

Paper Wraps

All it takes is a little imagination and some paper crafting supplies to create stunning soap wraps. From cigar bands to tied packages, these projects can be created in minutes.

- Craft glue
- Craft or double-sided tape
- Craft scissors
- Glue dots
- Paint brush: small
- Paper punches: various sizes
- Pencil
- Ruler

MATERIALS

- Decorative paper: various colors and weights
- Embellishments: metal shapes, stamps, etc.
- Ribbon or raffia

INSTRUCTIONS

1 Using the pencil and ruler, measure the soap and mark the decorative paper with the desired size, then cut out the shape using craft scissors.

2 Wrap the soap and adhere the ends of the paper using craft or double-sided tape.

3 Decorate the paper with embellishments and ribbon or raffia.

ABOUT THE AUTHOR

Rebecca Ittner was raised in California in a family where creativity was encouraged. Instead of staying inside watching television, she and her siblings played with clay, drew, painted with watercolors (or at least tried to), and, in general, made their own fun.

She is now a magazine and book editor, writer, photo stylist, and craft enthusiast. She says, "It took me a long time to figure out that I could do what I love and make a living at it. I am incredibly blessed." Rebecca's work has been featured in *Romantic Homes, Somerset Studio Take Ten, Somerset Home,* and *Somerset Life* magazines and many craft books. She also appeared on The Christopher Lowell Show.

To see more of Rebecca's work, visit rebeccaittner.etsy.com or read her blog at livelovecraft.com.

Acknowledgments

Thank you to my loving, supportive family. Mom, you are my hero. Your courage, strength, and unwavering love are the best gifts a mother could give. Debbie, Pete, and Perry, I am thankful for you every day.

Thank you to Peter, my rock and soft place to land. You make my life beautiful.

This book would not have been possible without the incredible team of women at Red Lips 4 Courage. Eileen, thank you for taking a chance on me all those years ago. I cherish your friendship. Cathy, thank you for your support and eagle eyes. I appreciate you more than you know. Erika, your courage and positive outlook always brighten my days. Thank you for spreading your sunshine. Your extra effort is greatly appreciated!

INDEX